Still More Activities That Teach

by Tom Jackson M.Ed.

Red Rock Publishing

Credits
Cover Design: Greg Bitney
Editing: Frank Jackson
Illustrations: Greg Bitney
Page Design and Typesetting: Accu-Type Typographers
Printing: Data Reproductions
First Printing 2000
Second Printing 2002

ISBN 0-9664633-5-8

Additional copies of this book and other materials by Tom Jackson
     may be ordered from your supplier or from:
Active Learning Center, Inc.
3835 West 800 North
Cedar City UT 84720
(435) 586-7058 between the hours of 7:00 a.m. and
     7:00 p.m. Mountain Time
FAX: (435) 586-0185
Toll free: 1-888-588-7078 between the hours of 7:00 a.m. and
     7:00 p.m. Mountain Time

Web site: www.activelearning.org
E-mail: staff@activelearning.org

**Have Tom Jackson speak to your organization or
conference. Call for information.**

CONTENTS

ABOUT THE AUTHOR
TOM JACKSON, M.ED.

Tom Jackson is an expert in the area of active learning. He has three previously published books, *Activities That Teach, More Activities That Teach* and *Activities That Teach Family Values*. His professional background includes a Master's Degree in Education from the University of Southern California. He spent 12 years as a high school social studies teacher in southern California. Tom spent the next 13 years as a prevention specialist for a mental health/alcohol and drug center in southwestern Utah. During his time with the state agency, he directed the prevention/education programs for five school districts and the surrounding communities. During this time, he also served as a member of the Utah State Office of Education's Curriculum Committee for Alcohol and Other Drug Education and on the Governor of Utah's Substance Abuse and Anti-Violence Coordinating Council.

In 1996 Tom was chosen as the Chemical Health Educator of the Year for the State of Utah. Then in 1997 he was awarded an Excellence in Outstanding Service to Education Award from the Utah State Board of Education. He has made guest appearances on a variety of radio and television programs as well as having a number of published articles.

Today, Tom Jackson is the director of the Active Learning Center, Inc. which distributes his activity books. He also directs the Active Learning Foundation, a nonprofit organization, which schedules speaking engagements around the country. Tom is a popular conference keynote, breakout and workshop presenter. He also conducts trainings for school districts and other organizations throughout the United States. His presentations have educated and entertained thousands of professionals, parents and youth across the country.

ACKNOWLEDGMENTS

I have been fortunate to be surrounded by caring and creative people. Books aren't created out of a vacuum and certainly this one is no exception. My former co-workers from Southwest Center and across the state of Utah are still very supportive of my efforts. The people that I meet on the road or that contact me by phone and e-mail are always willing to share their ideas and insights. Those individuals who were part of Tom's National Testers have encouraged me and provided valuable feedback on the activities in this book. My family is of course the foundation from which I work and my wife, Janet, is my strength. Three individuals have had to deal with the nuts and bolts of this book. My older son, Frank, has been my editor. He has the last word on what works and what doesn't. He is one smart kid, even if I do say so myself. If you find a mistake, it's because I didn't follow his instructions. A good friend, Greg Bitney, is the source of the illustrations and the cover of the book. He has the remarkable ability to bring to life, what I can only envision. My wife, Janet, takes care of everything. She is my sounding board, does the rough editing of the activities, handles the scheduling of my speaking presentations and takes care of the day-to-day operations of selling my books. No one could do it better than Janet. I love her lots. As always, God is the rock of my life!

TOM'S NATIONAL TESTERS

In the past I have always utilized friends to test my activities to see how they worked with varying groups. When I started putting this book together, I wanted to expand my testing group to include a wider variety of students. To accomplish this, I put out a call for volunteers who would be willing to take the drafts of my activities and see how they worked with their students. I received a number of applications from people who wanted to be part of this group that I was calling Tom's National Testers or TNT for short. I tried to choose people who worked with children and youth in varying demographic and economic areas. The individuals listed below worked with me through a two year testing process. Others who started helping me test had to drop out due to changes in teaching assignments or other mitigating circumstances. I have never met most of these people, but have become quite close through the medium of e-mail. I want to give each and every one of them a great big thank you for the efforts they made. Their suggestions were incorporated into the activities. At the end of some activities, you will find the phrase "TNT Idea". Here I have included a suggestion by one or more members of the group that is a variation on the activity. The activities and information you find in this book are better because of their involvement and commitment. Thank you one and all!

Laurel Avery-DeToy, lead teacher-mentor, Health Education, School of the Arts, Rochester, New York

Ann Banfield, Health Education, Naperville North High School, Naperville, Illinois

Robyn Barney, 4-H group leader, Weber County 4-H program, Roy, Utah

Guy Beard, Peer Helping & Psychology teacher, Pensacola High School, Pensacola, Florida

Jo Ann C. Chenell, Ph.D., Teen REACH and Project Discovery coordinator, Channahon, Illinois

Donna Clark, Life Management teacher, Manchester High School, Manchester, Michigan

Toni Cook, 6th grade teacher, William Penn Elementary, Salt Lake City, Utah

Thomas Corrigan, Prevention worker/Adolescent counselor at Crossroads, Mentor, Ohio

Debbie Deichelbohrer, 6th grade teacher, Christina Huddleston Elementary, Lakeville, Minnesota

Kara Dodds, 5th/6th grade multi-age teacher, Whittier Elementary School, Salt Lake City, Utah

Brenda Early, Counselor and PALS coordinator (high school/elementary mentoring program), Cabot High School, Cabot, Arkansas

Shirlie Freytag, Guidance counselor grades 5-8, Buchanan Middle School, Wray, Colorado

Ruth C. Gillmore, Home Economics teacher, Health & Peer Assistance Program, Covina High School, Temple City, California

Constance A. Gross, Family and Consumer Sciences teacher, South Webster High School, Wheelersburg, Ohio

Carrie Hale-Beauchamp, Health/Sociology teacher, Katy High School, Katy, Texas

Penny Judson, Special Education inclusion teacher in 5th and 6th grades, Christina Huddleston Elementary School, Lakeville, Minnesota

Katrina Larsen, School counselor, West Valley City, Utah

Tauna Larson, Educational Talent Search counselor, 21st Century Grant After School Program, Monticello, Utah

Keri Leinart, Skills for Living teacher, Ted Polk Middle School, Carrollton, Texas

Marcia Livingston, Family and Consumer Sciences teacher, North Union High School, Richwood, Ohio

Debbie Michaelis, 3rd - 4th grade teacher, Copper Hills Elementary, Magna, Utah

Lynn Mickelsen Dwyer, School social worker, Spicer Middle School, New London, Minnesota

Al Montgomery, retired high school principal, currently doing teacher training at the college level, Metairie, Louisiana

Randy Jo Nielsen, therapist, Horizon Adolescent Chemical Dependency Treatment Center, Fort Smith, Arkansas

Cathy O'Shea, Family and Consumer Sciences teacher, Meadville Area Sr. High School, Meadville, Pennsylvania

Craig Rasmussen, principal of an alternative high school, Sanpete Academy, Ephraim, Utah

Steve Sandman, K-8 School counselor, Buncombe County Schools, Black Mountain, North Carolina

Vince Seaman, Science Department chair, Chemistry teacher, El Camino High School, Sacramento, California

Gary Smith, School counselor, Washington Terrace, Marion Hills and Uintah Elementary Schools, Ogden, Utah

Janan Szurek, School social worker, Kendall County Special Education Cooperative - Boulder Hill Elementary School, Montgomery, Illinois

Holly Wamsley, Mathematics teacher, Hunter High School, West Valley City, Utah

Shannon Williams, 4-H assistant, Utah State University Extension, Monroe, Utah

Michelle L. Weltzin, prevention specialist, New Directions, Clinton, Iowa

Holly Woddard, Home Economics teacher, Abilene, Texas

Paul zumFelde, director of Lutheran Social Service, Western Region - N.W. Ohio, Archbold, Ohio

INTRODUCTION

This is my fourth book. In the first two, *Activities That Teach* and *More Activities That Teach,* I emphasized activities which would be used by people who worked in the classroom, in after school programs, with treatment or support groups, children and youth programs and church groups. This book is a continuation of that series. My third book, *Activities That Teach Family Values,* was written with families in mind. The activities in the family book allow a single parent with one child or a two parent family with lots of kids to join together and have fun while learning valuable lessons at the same time. However, since that book has been published, many teachers have taken the activities and adapted them for classroom use. For more information on the contents of these three books, please read their descriptions at the back of this book.

I have not repeated the opening chapters from the first two books in this volume. Those chapters deal in depth with the research behind why active learning is an effective teaching strategy and the nuts and bolts of how to lead a discussion. If you need this type of information, please refer to my first two books. In the opening chapters of this book, I have concentrated on other areas such as the importance of teaching life skills, how the acquisition of life skills can help kids, suggestions from active learning practitioners on how to effectively implement active learning lessons, success stories from the field (which I love) and an effective, yet simple, discussion outline. Of course, these are just a prelude to some great user-friendly activities you can use in your classroom or program.

At your request, I have added a number of new topics. Conflict resolution, respect, responsibility, school-to-careers, team building, media influence and healthy lifestyles are new areas you can explore with the activities in this book. I also hope you like the way I have divided the questions at the end of each activity into the "What", "So What" and "Now What" categories so it would be easier for you to follow that outline. It proved to be so popular in the family book that I used the same format in this one. Illustrations have also been added which should make some of the activities easier to understand.

I used a testing technique for the activities in this book that proved to be very useful. About two years ago, I put out a call for people who would like to test my activities before they were put into book form. A number of people responded and from those a group was chosen that represented a wide cross-section of people working with a variety of groups. This way I was able to receive feedback on how the activities worked with children and youth from across the country. Of that original group, some had to drop out due to changes in their assignments or other circumstances. However, a group of stalwart individuals went through the testing process with me and provided important feedback which made the activities you will find in this book very effective. I called this group Tom's National Testers, or just TNT for short. Their suggestions were incorporated into the activities. At the end of some activities, you will find the phrase "TNT Idea". Here I have included a suggestion by one or more members of the group that is a variation on the activity.

Please feel free to visit our web site at www.activelearning.org and provide me with any feedback about these activities, information you find that relates to the field of active learning, an activity idea you have or a success story of your own that you would like to share. The web site has a lot of interesting information that you will want to take a look at. While you are there, read the newsletter and sign up for the update which is e-mailed out whenever there have been significant changes on the web site. I hope you enjoy this book as much as you have the other ones. Above all, remember to have fun!

Chapter One

If We Can't Test It, Why Teach It?

We have all heard the battle cry, "We need to get back to basics. Let's just teach the three R's!" Well first of all, I have a tendency to worry about any movement which claims the three R's as their call to arms. You do realize that reading, writing and arithmetic don't all start with "R" don't you? Secondly, I must question the wisdom of such a simplistic approach. If national demographics and economic circumstances were the same today as they were fifty years ago, then this "back to basics" mantra might work. However, today we live in an increasingly complex society which requires us to address areas that have been called by many the "fourth R". This stands for responsibility and I find some comfort in the fact that at least it really does start with the letter "R". In my work with children and youth, I have included life skills such as decision making, communication, goal setting, conflict resolution, understanding others, substance abuse prevention, violence issues, problem solving, respect, working together, etc., as part of the fourth R.

Along with this back-to-basics movement, we are being bombarded with a demand for testing. Society wants to hold students accountable for their learning by measuring them against standards that have been set by a local school district or state office of education. Let me state for the record that as a former school teacher, a parent, a grandparent and one who has been working in the educational system since 1973, I am one hundred percent behind teaching kids to read, write and do arithmetic. Without these skills, all other efforts to help kids will fall short. These building blocks are definitely the cornerstone of education. I am not even against testing students to see where they stand in relation to where we expect them to be. Where I draw the line is in regards to reducing education to the point where we limit ourselves to teaching only the basics and then relying solely on standardized testing to measure our success. We cannot limit education to such a degree that we neglect giving our children and youth all of the tools they need to succeed in today's society. We must be watchful that educational reform does not result in such a single-minded obsession with testing that we forget the necessity of teaching the child in addition to teaching the lesson. We are not running factories, but schools. Students are not products which can easily be normed, meaned and averaged. They are people with individualized needs, strengths and aspirations who need to be taught a number of life skills in order to realize their dreams.

I feel that the acquisition of life skills is a basic requirement for all children. It is true that we don't have a multiple choice test to measure someone's decision making skills or their ability to set goals, but that doesn't make these skills any less important when we measure success. True success is measured by an individual's ability to assume their place in society and become a functioning, contributing member. This is the ultimate test of whether our schools have done their job or not. Any less of a standard must be counted as failure, whether students have passed a mandated test or not. An individual's acquisition of life skills has been shown to increase the odds of becoming a respected, contributing member of society. Without the fourth R, the first three R's will leave people living as a mere shadow of what they could become. Life skills must be included in every person's toolbox for them to have a chance to reach their full potential. Rather than continuing the polarizing debate between teaching only the basics or presenting an enriching curriculum that includes the fourth R, I would submit that we need to find a balance that mixes the two approaches and provides students with all of the necessary tools to succeed and contribute in today's fast paced and ever changing society.

Chapter Two

Life Skills: A Critical Component for Success

Eric Hoffer, a social philosopher, stated, "In times of change, learners inherit the earth while the learned find themselves beautifully equipped to deal with a world that no longer exists." I am sure that many of you have learned things that in later years have proven to be no longer of use. I spent two years in junior high school math learning how to use the slide rule. Today, you would be hard pressed to find a slide rule, much less a person under the age of thirty five who knows how to use one. The hand held calculator has made the slide rule and the ability to use it obsolete. Life skills, on the other hand, never go out of style. At a vocational conference I heard Jamie Vollmer, President of Vollmer and Associates, talking about education reform. He gave a very interesting statistic. He said, "For the children entering first grade this year (1997) 50% of the jobs that they will have in their lifetime have not yet been invented." I found that to be an astonishing statement that tells me that the children of today will have to be better prepared than past generations to meet the challenges of tomorrow. The Dean of the College of Letters, Arts & Sciences at the University of Southern California, Dr. Morton Owen Schapiro, talks about the same concept this way in the Winter 2000 issue of *The College*, "Students don't need training for today's realities as much as they need education for tomorrow's possibilities."

Horace Mann (1796 - 1859) was one of the early architects of America's public education system. He was a firm believer that schools should broaden their mandate to include "social efficiency, civic virtue and character." Today, I believe much of what he lobbied for could be included under the life skills umbrella. I met Dr. Sidney Simon, author of many books about education reform, at a weekend workshop in Philadelphia where he and I were both presenting. I was able to spend quite a bit of time with him discussing the needs of today's children and youth. He stated that, "Today's children are called upon to make decisions that yesterday's children were rarely called upon to make." Things move fast in today's society and problems that were formally only associated with high school age youth are now exhibiting themselves in middle and elementary age students. Examples of these would include acts of violence, gang membership, alcohol and drug use, sexual acting out, racial discrimination and a number of other issues.

Without the proper tools, our children will be seduced into anti-social behaviors without even realizing the extent of the danger involved or the possible consequences. These necessary tools include life skills such as decision making, communication, goal setting, media awareness, resistance to peer pressure, conflict resolution, understanding of others, substance abuse prevention, violence issues, problem solving, respect, working together, etc. Babies are not born with life skills. They need to be taught. I was walking down the street in Columbus, Ohio while presenting at a conference there. As I was walking, a man was coming towards me. He was still about fifty feet away when I noticed him. He was walking in such a way that he would bump into me if we both continued on our same paths. When we reached a distance of about fifteen feet apart, we both moved to our right and passed without incident. Now how did we both know that we should move to our right? It's simple: we were taught to pass on the right when learning how to drive. It wasn't knowledge that we brought into this world. (I have often wondered if this incident had happened in England, where they drive on the left side of the road instead of the right side, if both people would have moved to the left?) We can't assume that life skills are innate; they aren't! They need to be taught. If parents and schools don't teach life skills, who will? You can be sure that television, magazines, videos, video games, the internet and peers will fill the void. Do we wish the success of the next generation to be left to these sources? I would hope not!

Does the teaching of life skills make a difference? In the area of substance abuse, Dr. Gilbert Botvin, of Cornell University Medical College's Institute for Prevention Research, conducted a longitudinal, multi-year study that involved over 6,000 students which proved that life skills can reduce substance abuse. He first measured the drug use of randomly selected sixth grade students. Then he designated a control group and a group to which he taught life skills lessons in the seventh, eighth and ninth grades. When they were seniors, he once again measured their drug use. The group that had received the life skills lessons had up to a 64% lower rate of alcohol and other drug use than the group which did not receive the life skills training. The final conclusion of his research as summarized in the November 1994 issue of *Youth Update* was, "Prevention programs are most effective when they focus on life skills such as goal setting, decision making, friendship making, critical thinking and other such skills."

How about academic success? Search Institute has surveyed thousands of young people over the years and from that research has created a list of 40 developmental assets that will increase the likelihood of a person avoiding problems and achieving success. When looking at the list, many of the assets refer to areas of life skills. Search Institute concluded, "Academic success is related, in part, to students' social competence and their ability to adapt to different environments. Thus, the more equipped young people are to navigate life, the more they are likely to achieve in school." Another study by Alexander and Entwisle in 1988 came to this conclusion: "Research demonstrates that children's social competence influences their academic as well as their social performance." How well equipped our children and youth are in the area of life skills will have a direct influence on their academic performance. You want better test scores? Equip kids with better life skills!

Let's look at what role life skills can play in the workplace. I think that John D. Rockefeller summed it up best when he said, "I will pay more for the ability to deal with people than any other ability under the sun." In recent surveys, employers have noted time after time a need for employees with well developed life skills. In a survey reported in the newspaper USA Today on March 15, 1999, 51% of employers said their employees did not work well with others. In a survey conducted by the National Alliance of Business, communication skills and working in a team were listed as abilities that were missing in newly graduated students. In the June 26, 1997 issue of USA Today it was reported that only 13% of employers felt students just out of high school could work in diverse groups and they believed that only 6% to 9% of the students were able to communicate effectively. Margo Barnes, a senior vice president of Bayer Corporation, on July 7, 1997 in the USA Today stated, "The truth is that all companies will come to depend increasingly on a workforce equipped with critical thinking, problem solving and team working skills."

No matter what criteria you use to measure the importance of life skills, the result is the same. Without the acquisition of these important skills, an individual has greatly reduced their chances of success.

How should we teach life skills? My belief is that they should be taught by using active learning. We need to get our children and youth actively involved in their own learning process. A common refrain heard in schools is, "Is this going to be on the test?" William Glasser, author of a number of education related books including *The Quality School Teacher*, stated, "For many students the test has become much more important than what is learned." Since we do not take a test on communication or goal setting, we need to be sure that we use teaching strategies that will encourage retention of the information. Edgar Dale's Cone of Learning illustrates how by using different teaching strategies you can increase the rate of retention. Dale's research measured the percentage of information a student would retain when presented to them using different teaching strategies. As you can see by the diagram, teaching strategies which more fully engage the learner produced greater percentages of retention. A good lesson plan will incorporate a number of different teaching strategies which will not only increase retention, but also address a wide variety of learning styles.

Rate of Retention

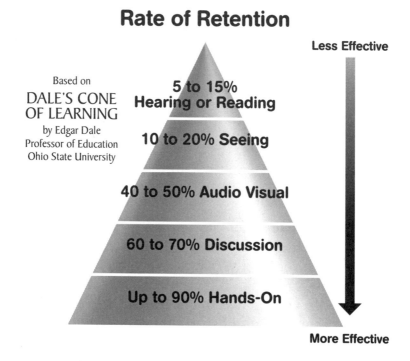

Less Effective

Based on
DALE'S CONE
OF LEARNING
by Edgar Dale
Professor of Education
Ohio State University

5 to 15% Hearing or Reading

10 to 20% Seeing

40 to 50% Audio Visual

60 to 70% Discussion

Up to 90% Hands-On

More Effective

Chapter Three

Using
Active Learning

Wouldn't you like to sit down and pick the brains of other people who have been using active learning? A time where you could ask the questions that have been bothering you? Sometimes spending just one hour with a person who has been using this type of teaching strategy can be more beneficial than weeks of trial and error experimentation on your own. Well I can't give you that one-on-one time, but I can give you the next best thing. At the beginning of this book I have listed a number of people who were part of Tom's National Testers, or as I called them, the TNT Group. Not only did these individuals test the activities found in this book, but I also asked some of the more experienced ones to share their expertise about active learning. If you would like to see what they teach, who they work with or where they are located, you may check the list at the front of the book. Here is a compilation of their practical, real-world suggestions covering three areas of common interest to those who use activities in their classrooms or programs. Some of their answers have been edited to save space. Remember that these are the opinions of various people who are involved in many different areas of serving children and youth. After you read what they have to say, it will be up to you to adapt their comments to meet your situation and needs.

What tips would you give to others about conducting an activity?

Be prepared and ready to go! If you take time to gather your materials at the beginning of class, you have already lost the students. Be enthusiastic! If you are not enthusiastic, how can the students care about participating. Read each activity carefully so you are familiar with what you need to do and what questions you will use in the processing. Ask yourself these questions: How will this activity integrate with my curriculum? How do I justify doing this activity in the classroom? How will I evaluate the students in terms of what they have learned? Connie Gross

Be prepared! Know the activity inside and out. If it doesn't go as planned - adjust. Have a sense of humor, this is not a chore. Tauna Larson

Be familiar with the activity and instructions before attempting it in front of a group for the first time. Do a dry run before you try it with your group. Double and triple check all your materials well before the start of your session. You can follow the activity outline exactly or make changes, even in mid-presentation. Craig Rasmussen

I feel that students need to be made aware of what the topic or focus of the activity is so they know the purpose. This will allow for a greater understanding of the activity. Make the students aware that you will be discussing the activity afterwards, so they know that they are expected to respond. If in the middle of an activity it begins to fail, either stop the activity or adapt it to make it work for the students. If activities like these have never been done in your classroom, it may take some time to get the kids used to it. Kara Dodds

Be patient and flexible. Sometimes your activity takes a totally different turn than intended but is equally valuable. And sometimes the first few activities that you try don't turn out the way you want. Keep trying! Practice makes perfect! Some activities work very well for some classes and not so great for other classes. Also listen. You learn a great deal about your students if you learn to listen to their responses and not just funnel the activity the direction you wanted it to go. Sometimes they need to go elsewhere. Holly Wamsley

Make sure you read all of the directions and get all of the equipment before doing an activity. Think about your group and make adaptations to the activity if needed before you do it so it will be successful. The activities are wonderful additions to the curriculum and can be adapted to fit many subjects. Robyn Barney

I like to have the group know that we will be doing another learning experience in a day or two. I have had a few parents come and comment on how their student has said "I have to go to school today because we are doing a learning experience and I want to be there." When that happens, you know the process is working. Gary Smith

Start small. Try out activities with only one class or group (the one you are most comfortable with) so you can fine tune the activity prior to springing it on more challenging groups. Play to teachable moments. I have done activities expecting the discussion to go in one direction when the kids took it in quite another. If I had insisted on bringing it back to my lesson plan before they finished with their direction, we all would have missed out on some great interactions. All activities should be considered "elastic". To be most effective they need to be stretched to fit you and your audience. Consider them recipes to be adjusted to your own individual style and taste. This seems pretty obvious to some people, but it took me the longest time to realize that adapting someone else's work was a good thing to do and enhanced rather than detracted from what they had done. Don't be afraid to be childish with middle school and high school age students. Some activities that may seem childish to you will be favorably received by these audiences and often result in the best discussions because it gives them permission to be more child-like and therefore open. Shirlie Freytag

Smile. Know your students so the activity will fit their needs, not yours. You take charge; don't let them boss the group around. Know what you are doing. Don't read the activity from the book as you go along. Relax and enjoy. If the activity doesn't go quite like you planned, talk about the activity and the expectations and see what went different. Putting up bulletin boards on the activities is a good way to reinforce the activity. Tauna Larson

Take into consideration how each class is different. Evaluate the levels and behaviors of each class and plan accordingly. Carrie Hale-Beauchamp

Go for it! Active learning puts you in an awkward

position sometimes because you may not be comfortable leading these types of activities. Not only will the experience give you confidence to do more, but it brings you down to the level of the students - trying new things and being uncomfortable in the school system. I find that not only do my students enjoy the activities, learn something new, think about things in a new way, but I also grow because I remember how it feels to be in the position my students are in. Trying new things forces us to think about how we are doing things in our classrooms. Yes, it puts you in a vulnerable position, but that is exactly where you can grow as a professional. Steve Sandman

Be thoroughly familiar with the activity by reading through it several times. Sometimes I tell the students what the topic is for the day and have them try to figure out how the activity relates instead of giving them all of the background information before beginning. This way they work at thinking about it and making the connection themselves. This makes it more personal and they come up with amazing things I would never think of. Katrina Larsen

One of the biggest tips is to keep the activity relevant and simple. Have an open mind and do not expect the activity to run perfectly. No matter how much you prepare, something can always happen - just go with it and use it when you process with the students. Ann Banfield

Always allow enough time for processing. There is no purpose in doing the activity without processing it. Do not allow the students to ask too many questions regarding the activity after you have explained it. This takes away from them taking responsibility for problem solving, cooperation and brainstorming. If you aren't the regular classroom teacher, make sure the teacher is involved. They know their students' personalities and needs. They can help guide the discussion in appropriate directions. Janan Szurek

How do you deal with teachers or administrators that think activities are just "play time"?

The only times I've had a teacher or administrator think it was play time occurred when they had not seen the full activity. I find it useful to have them observe the full activity (discussion and all). If they are still not a believer, I have them watch while I review past activities with the students. Asking them what were their favorite activities and why. Then the clincher: I ask what they were learning about by doing the activity. They know and they remember! Katrina Larsen

Usually this can be dealt with by an adequate, yet simple explanation and description of the activity, its intent and its outcome. For the very resistant, I invite them to come and observe, even participate if they would like. Guy Beard

I have lead by example. I do a pilot program in one class and it catches on. Find one supportive teacher willing to give it a try and you will be surprised how others jump on the bandwagon. Make sure that all of your activities have a lesson to be taught! Janan Szurek

If teachers question it, I ask them to come in or let me go to their class to do an activity. They have a chance to see how valuable it is and then I have them coming to me to get ideas. My principal is wonderful and has come in while we do activities. I have even done them in faculty meetings so teachers can get a feel for them and how they can be used in a classroom. The response has been great! Debbie Michaelis

Everyone here at the treatment center supports the activities, however it should be clear that the major advantage for adolescents is it helps them move from concrete thinking to abstract thinking. The activities may look like play, but using these tools can help children through very serious and important living and thinking transitions. Randy Jo Nielsen

Most of my students will never use higher math again after high school, or at the most, college. The activities teach values that should and will be used all of their lives. My job is not to just educate the mathematical part of the person. My job is to educate the whole person! We still get through the required material in all of my classes, but the activities make them more responsive to me and more willing to do math. It also lets me better understand my students so that I am better able to teach in such a way that they understand and learn. Holly Wamsley

If administrators or other staff members think that my activities are just play time, I do not argue my point. I simply invite them into my classroom to view one. This way they can experience my activities and see all the different kinds of learning taking place. The activity is not solely about the intended topic, but about cooperative work, social skills, support and respect, and enjoying learning. I also invite that staff member to stick around and listen to the processing that follows. When this person hears the discussion, they will realize that the activities have merit. Ann Banfield

I believe the key here is relationships. It is always hard to sell somebody something. But if they see that the kids enjoy it and then you show them that the students learned something, they start getting interested. Steve Sandman

I have not found administrators who understand what the objectives of these activities are to consider it "play time". I have found that with a wee bit of prior education of how learning occurs best, that all have been very receptive . In fact, they are proud when they hear students talking about what they did in Mrs. Avery-DeToy's health class. Laurel Avery-DeToy

Some teachers and administrators are reluctant to do active learning because they feel they are giving up control of the class to the students. I contend that teachers must "give up" the responsibility for learning to their students before youth will actively become involved in the learning process. Paul zumFelde

The elementary teachers and administrators are much more accepting because they see the changes the activities are making in the students' lives. When kids are in high school, changes are harder to see. High school people are more curriculum based, but with all the tragedies around the country they are now more open to anything that can help. Brenda Early

Our school secretary has a fit if we have to cancel our activity days for any reason because she knows that all children will be present and on time on activity day. If they are tardy, they cannot participate; therefore, they are not tardy and rarely absent on Thursdays. It is not play time due to the processing that changes it from just a game to a learning, bonding time. Toni Cook

I call the activities "learning experiences" instead of activities because they involve so many different learning styles. Our school is focused on teaching kids in the learning style that best meets their needs. Gary Smith

How often do you use activities?

I use the activities when they "feel right" - I know that's not a very scientific response, however, teachers know when they fit in "just right". I try to use at least two a week, however, sometimes it's less or more depending on where the last topic in health takes us. Laurel Avery-DeToy

How many you can do before students get tired of activities will depend on how well you do the activity and how bored they have been by the presentation style of you and other teachers prior to this activity. Craig Rasmussen

I recommend using these activities at least once a week. Every class has a busy schedule, but if you agree to do an activity once a week on a certain day, at a certain time, it becomes a part of the routine and gives the students something to look forward to. If this is not possible, I would encourage every teacher to try using activities at least once a quarter. Kara Dodds

I try to use them once a week or when introducing a new chapter. Carrie Hale-Beauchamp

Whenever there is a slow ten minutes. Shannon Williams

The average for me is usually two times a week. It

creates energy in the room and it not only motivates the students...it motivates me! Ann Banfield

I use activities to introduce a new topic/concept, to illustrate a concept in a more concrete way, to break up a long training session, to re-focus the class or to "smooth ruffled feathers" when I discern disharmony in the class. The actual timing varies because of the nature of the material. I like to use activities on a random basis so the students do not get into an "expecting" routine. Guy Beard

I do a number of activities during the first three weeks of school. After that I use them about once a week. Debbie Michaelis

At least twice a week in the beginning of the school year and then once a week. Al Montgomery

I use the activities once or twice a month. Since they are not a part of my chemistry curriculum, I use them to give students a break from the chemistry, especially if there is something going on locally or in the school that relates to one of the activities. Vince Seaman

Four Easy Steps to a Great Discussion

You have just conducted a great activity. All of your kids were involved, interested and the energy level was high. However, as soon as you start leading a discussion about how the activity might relate to real life issues, those same involved kids become silent as a sphinx. This scenario is all too real for many people who work with children and youth. Those who use active learning as a teaching strategy really like it, but to be truly effective the discussion dilemma must be solved. This chapter won't address all of the issues surrounding how to lead a discussion, but it will give you a basic outline to follow during the discussion time. More information about leading discussions can be found in both of my first two books *Activities That Teach* and *More Activities That Teach*.

Over the past number of years I have utilized a four step process that has allowed me to effectively conduct a discussion with kids. This process has worked whether the kids are gifted, run of the mill or part of the high risk population. The first three steps are centered around the questions that you ask, and the final step is a tool for the teacher or leader to condense all of what has been discussed and put it into a neat package.

The first step involves asking "What" questions. No this doesn't mean that every question has to start with "what". It means that the questions all relate to what happened during the activity. These questions can be open or closed ended questions. They don't look for any great insights from the students nor are they a major part of the teaching process. However, the "What" questions do serve a valuable purpose. They are used to get kids to start talking. As discussion leaders we want to quickly get to the heart of the issue and begin to explore the critical answers that will hopefully bring about a change in the lives of our students. Unfortunately, the kids are usually not as motivated as we are. Therefore you need to prime the pump a little to get them engaged.

The "What" questions allow the students to begin talking. The questions are easy enough to answer that everyone will have a response. One of the mistakes that I see some discussion leaders commit is starting the questions at a level that requires too much personal risk or revealing information when responding. Questions that ask for a response about how a person felt emotionally or how this activity relates to things that are happening in their lives requires some commitment from the students. If you begin a discussion by asking the students to offer their opinion, you are many times met with a stony silence. When a discussion begins with long periods of silence, the leader feels disheartened and brings the discussion to an end rather quickly. When you start with easy questions that everyone can answer and that puts them at very little risk when responding, the discussion is off to an energetic start and can build from there.

The second step is to ask "So What" questions. These are questions about what the activity has to do with real life issues in the context of your lesson plan. Remember that the students aren't doing the activity without it being a part of a larger lesson plan. They know that the topic for today is stress, goal setting, communication, conflict resolution, etc. and therefore have a context in which to place the activity. From this context, they can make comparisons about what happened during the activity with what can happen in real life. The "So What" questions are the heart of the discussion. It is during this portion of the discussion that you can ask for student opinions and have a free flowing exchange of ideas. The questions that you ask will hopefully lead the students to the pro-social concept that you want to teach. If the questions that you are asking do not bring about this desired response, then rephrase your questions and keep asking. If the student comments move the discussion in a direction you hadn't planned on, simply decide how much time you can allow for "off topic discussion". You can always pull the discussion back on track by asking a question that brings them back to the topic at hand. Don't be too quick to get back on topic. Many times the topics the students want to discuss are important issues to them. This second step will probably be the one that you will spend the most time on.

During the third step you ask "Now What" questions. Here you are asking questions that you hope will lead to behavior or attitude changes that can impact their lives. Since we use activities as a teaching strategy, there must be a point to why we did the activity. It is during this third step that we make sure the objective of the activity comes across loud and clear. The questions we ask during this part of the discussion are the ones which lead the students to understand how the pro-social attitude or behavior that the lesson is about can be implemented in their lives. This portion of the discussion will not last very long since you are no longer trying to relate the activity to your lesson plan, but rather you are reinforcing the message or messages that you discussed during the "So What" step.

At the end of each activity I have listed a number of questions you can ask during each of these three steps. However, understand that I have usually listed more questions than you need to use. I did this to give you an opportunity to pick and choose ones that would best fit your group or the concept that you wanted to address. My questions give you some insight into what I was thinking when I wrote the activity. You do not need to use these exact questions; you may make up your own. You should always add some questions that relate specifically to how your group responded to the activity. These questions will personalize the discussion.

The fourth step involves summarization. It is your opportunity to remind the students of what was talked about. You can emphasize the answers that support your pro-social message and leave out those that were off the mark or comments that were repetitive. The summarization is an opportunity to once again reinforce the objective of your lesson plan. I have found two things that are worth mentioning. Students tend to remember what was said by an authority figure and they tend to remember what was said last. Both of these factors are beneficial to you as the leader of the discussion. You are the authority figure since you are the one in charge, and by putting yourself in the position of summarizing, you will be the one that they hear last.

Let's review the process. During the first step you engage the students and get them involved in the discussion. The second step allows you to ask for opinions from the students and have them apply what took place during the activity to the topic you are addressing. The third step focuses the discussion on specific attitudes or behavior changes that could be made considering the comments from step two. The fourth and final step is a general summary where you reinforce what was said in steps two and three and apply those comments to your lesson plan. I have found this four step outline to be simple enough that I can easily use it to be sure that the discussion is on track and meeting my teaching needs. Too many times I hear people say that when the discussion is over, they aren't sure if they got their point across. By going through these four steps, you can guide the discussion in such a way that your objectives will be met. One, two, three, four - practice it a few times and you too will have great discussions.

Chapter Five

Let's Celebrate!

When something good happens we need to celebrate! The Active Learning Foundation has received story after story celebrating the benefits of using active learning with children and youth. These stories have come from every geographical area of the country and represent groups in rural, suburban and urban settings. They depict a wide range of groups from gifted programs to adjudicated programs and everything else you can think of. Some stories are about kids in classrooms, while others talk about after school programs, church groups, camps, clubs, support and treatment groups, etc. You will be reading about real kids in real situations, written by the people who were there. The hardest part for me was choosing which stories to leave out so there would still be room for new activities. The stories have been edited to conserve space. As you read the accounts of how lives have been impacted, you will feel the excitement and the thrill of active learning. Even though there is a lot of research to substantiate the use of activities, I think these stories show what happens when research meets the real world.

I am a school counselor working with grades K-8. I did the activity called "M&M Madness" (found in *More Activities That Teach*) with fifth graders and tried to focus on the aspect of peer pressure. A couple of weeks later I was talking to a girl that was struggling with the temptation to smoke with her friends. It would have been easy for me to lecture her or preach to her, but I resisted. I did however, remind her of the M&M activity. We compared the activity to her situation with smoking and she was very convicted. I didn't have to say that smoking was a bad choice or tell her not to do that. She realized that those friends were trying to get her to "change her guess" and she knew that she was right in the first place. It was an awesome experience of self discovery for her and I have a feeling that it went a lot further than a lecture from me. Galileo said it best, "You can not teach people anything, you can only help them discover it themselves."

Steve Sandman
Black Mountain, North Carolina

*   *   *

I teach high school health in a suburb of Chicago. The majority of my students are affluent, so my activities have to be "cool" to catch their attention. Your activities have certainly met that need. Let me explain. We have our kids write a letter to themselves at the end of our semester together. The letters have certain points to cover and one point is to write about something you learned in Health class that you never want to forget. Numerous times these students have referred to a topic and then also made reference to the activity that accompanied it. The kids get the letters in the mail right before they graduate and they can still come by and tell me about the activities we did two years prior. These activities are priceless. I would not be an effective teacher without my active learning strategies. It is so rewarding to see the students have fun and learn at the same time.

Ann Banfield
Naperville, Illinois

*   *   *

I teach high school math. I use the results from some of the activities we do in the statistics sections of my classes. Every year as part of my final exam I ask, "What is the most important non-mathematical thing you learned during the year?" Almost every single student I have responds with something they learned from an activity I have done in class. They tell how it has affected their lives and their choices. We are making better young people by giving them a chance to learn values through these activities. I have had several students come back in later years and talk about an activity. They are remembering and truly learning.

Holly Wamsley
Salt Lake City, Utah

*   *   *

For the past six months we have used active learning strategies in our sixth grade inclusion classroom. The class has twenty-five gifted students, learning disabled students, students with behavioral disorders as well as so called average students. "Group activities" have been the most popular thing we've done all year.

These activities have taught our students how to get along. This may sound trite until you realize that the students who would previously dominate groups, have learned to listen to input from all group members. Our most quiet learning disabled student feels confident enough to tell her group what she thinks they should try. All of the students have started to think outside of the box - trying one solution to a problem and, if it doesn't work, trying something else. They are learning that it is OK to learn from your mistakes. We find them talking about ideas and planning before they try something. The debriefing questions at the end of each activity enhance the learning process, ensuring carry over into real life. One time a substitute teacher presented one of these activities and did not use the debriefing questions. Students asked, "Hey, wait a minute. What was the lesson of this activity?"

Penny Judson
Lakeville, Minnesota

*   *   *

I work in the 4H program and firmly believe in hands-on learning. What I find amazing is even after a month, the youth can remember the activity and its meaning. Sometimes they even come up with new applications for the activities on their own. I also find that I prepare better when I use an activity, so the lesson is more focused. My kids remember an activity for a long time, so the learning time spent on the activity is more productive.

Robyn Barney
Roy, Utah

*   *   *

As an elementary guidance counselor, I run parent education workshops to help families integrate what we are teaching here at school into the home environment. In my parent presentations I use many of your "hands on activities" to teach the parents how they can talk and discuss situations concerning "the right choice to make" with their kids and really have them listen! Parents shared that they liked the idea of an "activity" to teach the value or right choice to be made, because it took the heat off them to talk the whole time.

Lisa Miller
Lorain, Ohio

* * *

As a school counselor and a church youth director, I have had the opportunity to incorporate many lessons from the books *Activities That Teach* and *More Activities That Teach*. We recently completed two activities that focused on diversity. I believe that both activities helped our youth be more accepting of people from different races, cultures, ethnic groups, and socioeconomic groups. The youth responded to the activities by making a resolution to be considerate of others who are different from themselves.

Stephanie Holcomb
Birmingham, Alabama

* * *

I am a grade 8 health educator. I was introduced to active learning in 1998 by my sponsor teacher. Frankly, I survived my first year of teaching because of my confidence and success with active learning. I have completely incorporated active learning strategies into my curriculum. When doing the activities, the looks on the students' faces are priceless. I feel as if I am able to see the light bulbs turn on during our discussion session after the activity. I love when we are in the midst of the activity and I hear, "What is the point of this?" They always answer their own question during our discussion. Though I am still a "rookie", I believe in the advantages of active learning. It is not only fun and educational for the students, but it is refreshing to see students so thoroughly engaged and excited about their learning experiences.

Suzanne Beliveau
Coral Springs, Florida

*   *   *

Activities allow critical thinking to be practiced, developed, and become a part of the daily thinking process. Appropriate sayings to describe the active learning process would be "The light just came on", "It clicked", "He's got it, by George!" and "What an Ah ha experience!"

Randy Jo Nielsen
Fort Smith, Arkansas

*   *   *

I am currently the DARE/GREAT Instructor for our police department. During the course of the year I find myself giving many talks about drugs, violence, decision-making, etc., to the young people of our community. I have found that using active learning activities has made a big difference in the way the presentations are received. I found that if you stand and just lecture to kids for 45 minutes to an hour they will lose interest and the information is not well received. I have personally found that by seeing a demonstration of something or actually trying something myself, I learn more and remember more. The kids are the same way. The kids find the activities fun and exciting while still learning valuable information. I am always having kids talk about one of the activities that I demonstrated to them during a presentation. The kids get very excited about being involved in the demonstration. I have found that no matter how shy a kid may be or how cocky a kid may act, when you do a fun activity they get all excited and want to participate. Activities truly help teach not only young people, but adults, important skills and information through visual effects.

Rick Crossen
Athens, Ohio

*   *   *

I deal mostly with adolescent offenders in a prevention/intervention organization. At parenting classes which include youth, I do the activity called "Cover Up" (found in *Activities That Teach Family Values*). It deals with honesty. After explaining the activity, I have an adolescent and parent come up and try it. First the adolescent tries their luck. After a few attempts the frustration kicks in. I then I ask the parent to try it. Sometimes I get a parent who believes that their child just did not use the right technique. They soon realize how difficult it is and then you learn where the youth gets some of their behaviors of expressing frustration.

I then start with the questions. Everyone is usually

smiling at this point. One of the questions I ask the parent is if they had ever covered up for their child by lying to a probation officer or school official. Most of the time they believe they are doing it out of love and protection. The look on their faces is not of shame, but of realization. They had never realized that certain behaviors they believe to be innocent, like lying, can create such a big problem. We also discuss that when their child sees them lie to others, they get the message that it is okay to lie as well. We then discuss the value of honesty and how to rebuild trust in the family.

The use of this activity is invaluable. It assists in discussing topics in a non-threatening way and offers parents insight into how much their adolescent pays attention to them.

Sandra H. Sada
Corpus Christi, Texas

*   *   *

My work as a school social worker has afforded me many opportunities to incorporate active learning strategies. Last year I taught a life skills group for a high school special education classroom. Activities that illustrate positive life skills in a fun and interesting way really engage the learner. Often simply talking about the issues was not effective due to their limited ability to think abstractly. But give them an activity and watch what happens! My group was able to remember the topic from week to week, due to having concrete examples which helped them to internalize the learning. Best of all, once the topic was illustrated by the activity, the students were more willing to discuss the problems they face and the successes they experience. Activities aid in the development of insight and encourage the student to be part of his or her own learning process.

Alison Metz, MSW
Waterman, Illinois

* * *

As a junior high school counselor, I cannot express the importance of active learning enough. In the past our school has had a reputation of gangs, drugs, and violence, but through character education and active learning we have been able to begin to shift the stereotype that has been placed on our school. We have been able to use these activities to supplement materials, introduce topics, and add emphasis to ideas. For those who haven't tried it, a small hands-on activity can make a world of difference.

Mistalyn Leis
Utah

* * *

I am an elementary school counselor. I have used the activity called "Back Art" (found in *Activities That Teach*) over and over again with my 3rd to 5th grade students and it is such an "Ah ha" experience. The kids find this simulation so applicable to many situations in life, but especially as it relates to gossip. After they experience the simulation, the lesson practically teaches itself. The teachers at my school tell me that this lesson really slows down many of the little girls and their "secret" messages to one another. It also really helps our kids think about what they say before they say it. I find kids being much more complimentary of each other after the lesson.

Terri Key
Morton, Texas

*   *   *

Currently, I am in my third year of teaching Family and Consumer Sciences. I have found that students absolutely love these activities. Of course, they don't want to listen to me lecture the whole class period. The activities provide transitional and /or supplemental learning material. The thing is, it is learning fun! The kids want to do these activities and the questions provide in-depth discussions. It helps them learn about themselves, skills of teamwork, and relating to others.

Jennifer Church
Liberty, Indiana

*   *   *

Just wanted you to know that my students finally understood the process of oxidation after I did your activity "Liver Failure" (found in *More Activities That Teach*). The activity uses a sponge to demonstrate how your liver oxidizes alcohol. In prior years they just read the material from the chapter which describes oxidation, now they have a visual image. Much more effective!

Carrie Hale-Beauchamp
Katy, Texas

*   *   *

We work as Family Teachers for a youth treatment program. Our job is to teach our youth how to interact in a family setting, hence the name Family Teachers. We run a group home for adolescent youth; it is our work and our home. As an intensive therapy unit we need to break away from the stress of "dealing with our issues" and have fun through active learning experiences. By participating in these activities we have built strong enduring relationships with our foster youth.

Layne and Lynnette Daybell
Kearns, Utah

*   *   *

I felt very satisfied when a parent told me, "My child enjoys being a part of your class because you make learning fun." When one teaches "life skills", it's often difficult to get students to understand how feelings and emotions impact their lives. Many teens do not like "touchy/feely" subjects. The active learning activities make teaching those hard subjects a little less threatening and fun too!

Ruth Gillmore
Temple City, California

*   *   *

I teach Family and Consumer Sciences. I use active learning and have found it to be more easily remembered than lectures or book learning (passive learning). It also gets the students up and moving around - it brings fun and uniqueness to my teaching and to their learning! Activities break down the cliques and barriers between students. Bonding can take place! Here are some comments from students in my classes. "I learned a lot more by doing this activity than from reading a book." "It makes a lot more sense to learn this way." "Activities make me stop and think."

Connie Gross
Wheelersburg, Ohio

*   *   *

I think one of the greatest benefits of doing the various activities is how the class comes together. Another benefit is the dawning of insight as a result of participating in what on the surface may seem like an unrelated activity - the "Ah ha" moment. I love to hear after class, "Mr. Beard, that was a really neat activity." The most difficult part of conducting an activity is deciding which one to do!

Guy Beard
Pensacola, Florida

*   *   *

If you have any stories you would like to share concerning how active learning has impacted or benefited the children and youth you work with, please share them with us. We would love to hear from you! You can mail them to Active Learning Foundation, 3835 West 800 North, Cedar City, UT 84720 or e-mail them to us at staff@activelearning.org

Chapter Six

Active Learning Lesson Plans

"More knowledge is gained from making the map than following the map!"

Dave Kastberg
Geography teacher at Ellsworth High School in Wisconsin

"My students really enjoy being able to partici-pate in the activities and retain a lot more through active learning than they would through lectur-ing."

Angela Radde
Counselor at Whitney Elementary School in Texas

"Within weeks of starting to use your active learning lesson plans, I began to see my students processing the activities earlier and earlier in the lesson and coming up with awesome insights."

Gail Ramp, Program coordinator
at the Council on Alcohol and Drug Abuse in Waco, Texas

"I absolutely grin with pleasure every time we use one of your activities and the students "get the point".

Cherie Coccia
Guidance counselor in Orange City, Florida

ALPHABET SOUP

TOPIC AREA: Alcohol, Drugs

CONCEPT: Alcohol and other depressant drugs slow down the thinking process. Decision making is slowed and reaction time is decreased when someone is impaired. This impairment can lead to problems when complex situations are encountered or quick reactions are required. As an example, let's look at driving a car. Traveling at 60 miles per hour, a car will cover 88 feet in one second. If the driver has been impaired by alcohol or another depressant drug and takes an additional one second to move his or her foot from the accelerator to the brake then they have increased their risk of hitting another car or object by 88 feet. This is an unacceptable risk on today's crowded highways. It also points out why an impaired driver is at a much greater risk to be in an accident compared with the average driver. Driving is just one example. Any task that requires making quick decisions or fast reaction time will be similarly affected.

METHOD: Classroom activity

TIME ESTIMATE: 4 minutes plus discussion time

MATERIALS NEEDED: None

ACTIVITY: Have everyone get with a partner. Explain that you are going to call out a letter of the alphabet. Each person will compete against their partner to see who can say the next letter of the alphabet first. For example, you will call out the letter "f". The first person in each pair that says "g" will receive five points. If they tie, no points are awarded. Stop long enough after you call out each number so the pair can keep track of their score. Quickly repeat this about ten times using different letters each time.

In round two explain that the rules are changing. Now instead of saying the letter that comes after the letter that you call out, they must say the letter that comes before the letter you call out. For example, you will call out the letter "f". The first person in each pair that says "e" will receive the five points. Repeat this about five times using different letters each time.

DISCUSSION IDEAS:

"What" Questions
- How well did you do in round one?
- How well did you do in round two?
- What was your total score?
- Why was round one easy?
- What made round two more difficult?

"So What" Questions
- How can we compare this activity to trying to do something while under the influence of alcohol or drugs?
- What types of actions do you do everyday that would be affected by alcohol or other drugs?
- How would being impaired by alcohol or other drugs affect you if you were driving a car?
- What occupations would be dangerous if you were doing them while impaired?
- How can someone else being impaired affect you?

- Why is it important to be educated about the affects of alcohol and other drugs?

"Now What" Questions
- What can you do to avoid situations where you would be harmed by someone who is impaired?
- How can you help others from becoming impaired?

BE ALL YOU CAN BE

TOPIC AREA: Self-Esteem, Suicide

CONCEPT: The Army has an advertising slogan that says "Be all you can be". Unfortunately a lot of our kids are trying to be all that someone else is. They try to be someone else instead of the best "them" that they can be. As they try to live up to unrealistic expectations, they set themselves up for failure. Every basketball player isn't going to be Michael Jordan, every student isn't going to have a straight "A" report card, every person's body isn't going to look like the ones on the pages of a magazine, but every person can be the best at being themselves. Once we stop trying to be someone else, we can devote more time to exploring and improving ourselves. Much of the dissatisfaction that many kids feel comes from when they compare themselves to someone else.

METHOD: Classroom activity

TIME ESTIMATE: 10 minutes plus discussion time

MATERIALS NEEDED:
• A watch with a second hand

ACTIVITY: Have your group stand or sit in a circle. Explain that their challenge is to go around the circle as quickly as possible with each person saying their first name. You will time them as they do it. Repeat this about three times to see if they can get faster. For the next round change the challenge slightly. This time they must say the name of the person on their left. Once again repeat this a couple of times to see if their speed can increase. For the third round have them think of a cartoon character or sports person. The person they choose does not have to be of the same gender as they are. As they go around the circle this time, have them say the cartoon character or sports figure's name. Once again repeat a couple of times to see if they can increase their speed.

DISCUSSION IDEAS:

"What" Questions
- How fast did we end up going when we used our own names?
- How fast did we end up going when we used our neighbor's name?
- How fast did we end up going when we choose a cartoon or sports figure?

"So What" Questions
- Why could we say our own names faster than the names of someone else?
- How easy is it for us to look like someone else?
- What makes it hard for us to act like someone else?
- What makes each person unique?
- How can comparing ourselves to others slow down our own personal growth?
- How hard is it to not compare ourselves to others?
- In what areas do we find ourselves comparing ourselves to others?
- Why do you think the Army used the phrase "Be all you can be"?
- Is anyone the best at all things? Explain.

- Should we stop trying to accomplish something just because we aren't number one? Why or why not?

"Now What" Questions
- How is comparing ourselves to others the wrong thing to do?
- How can we be the best "us" that we can be?

BEYOND PASS RIGHT - PASS LEFT

TOPIC AREA: Communication

CONCEPT: One of the most important skills needed for good communication is the skill of listening. This activity will show the importance of listening and how difficult that is when you are not concentrating on what is being said because you are busy doing something else. If you enjoyed the activity "Pass Right - Pass Left" with the Wright Family in my first book, *Activities That Teach*, then you have to give this one a try.

METHOD: Classroom activity

TIME ESTIMATE: 10 minutes plus discussion time

MATERIALS NEEDED:
• 1 small object per person such as a button or a coin

ACTIVITY: (*You will need at least nine people to make this activity work.) Give each person a small object that they can hold easily. Have everyone line up in three equal rows, with one line being behind the other. (See figure 1) It doesn't matter how long each row is. But each row needs to have the same number of people in it. If you do not have the correct number of people to make equal rows, you have a few options. You may have the leftover person read the story, you may join in and participate or you may rotate the extra people in and out of the activity. In my opinion, the last option is the best choice. The story pauses three times during the reading for rotation. At each rotation, have someone come out of the activity and have your extra people rotate in.

Begin to read the story. Each time the word left, right (or Wright), back or front are used, have each person pass one object to the person who is that direction from them. The key is that you must pass your object and receive an object at the same time. If you are holding more than one object, you only pass one not both. If you do not have a person next to you in the direction that is read, then you hold onto the object that you have. You would still accept an object, but you wouldn't pass one. For example the first row would not be able to pass their object to anyone when the word front is read since there is not a row in front of them but they would accept an object from the person behind them. Likewise the person at the end of each row could not pass their object a certain direction when there was no one next to them. At

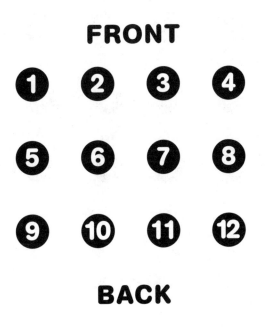

Fig. 1

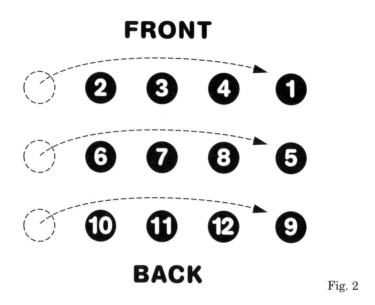

Fig. 2

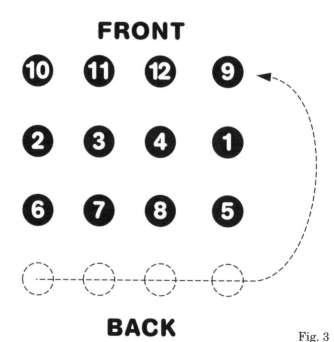

Fig. 3

the end of each paragraph stop reading and have everyone rotate in the following manner: The person at the left end of each line goes to the right end of the line and everyone moves over one space. (See figure 2) Then the back row moves to the front and each row moves back thereby moving the middle row to the back and the front row to the middle. (See figure 3) At the end of each paragraph every person should be holding one button. If that is not the case, then someone missed a direction here or there. If necessary, redistribute the buttons so everyone begins the next paragraph with a button.

Another Day With The Wright Family

One day Father Wright had to go to work earlier than usual. He left the house but had to go back inside because he had forgotten his coat which was in the very back of the closet. Just after he left the house, Mother Wright called to him to come in again because he had forgotten to shut the front door. Once he had shut the front door he was headed off to work.

Before he could even get a few feet from the front door, he tripped over some toys that had been tossed around the yard. He turned back around and yelled for the Wright children to gather in the living room. All of the children left what they were doing and hurried in. One of the children had to run up stairs to get her favorite toy that she had forgotten back on the floor. They were all now standing in front of their father. "Who left all the toys where I might trip over them?" Father Wright asked. None of the children admitted that their toys were in the yard. After much discussion, they left to go to their rooms and the parents went to look at the mess in the Wright family's yard.

As they viewed the mess in the front yard, they wondered about what the back yard looked liked. Sure enough there were toys on the right side of the yard and there were even more toys spread all over the left side of the yard. It might have been worse than the front yard. They called the children back into the living room and told them that the back yard was a mess and they couldn't leave it like that. Everyone went to the front yard to take another look and see how many toys were still in the yard. Father Wright tripped over a bucket full of water and the water left a large stain on his shirt. He should have left to go to work by now, but he had to go right in the house and change his shirt.

As Father Wright went through the door one of the children asked what had left the stain on his shirt. He was too busy trying to get back on schedule to answer any questions about what was on the front of his shirt. While all of this was going on, Mother Wright was cooking breakfast. Things had been so crazy that she had left the stove on and had burned the bacon. She left the room when she saw smoke coming out of the kitchen. Mother Wright screamed for everyone to run out the front door and gather in the yard. It was a good thing that all of the toys were put back where they belonged or someone might have tripped over them. With all of the problems, Father Wright decided that it would be a good time to take a vacation so he loaded up the family and left.

DISCUSSION IDEAS:

"What" Questions
* How hard was it to keep up with the story?

- How easy was it to get the object in and out of your hand?
- What problems did you have when passing the object?
- What would have made the activity easier to accomplish?

"So What" Questions
- How did you feel during the activity?
- What impact did other's actions have on your ability to stay up with the story?
- How hard was it to listen and pass the objects at the same time?
- How much of the story can you remember?
- How hard were you concentrating on the story during the activity?
- How hard were the people around you concentrating on the story?
- What role does concentration play in communication?
- What can we do to improve our concentration skills?
- Describe a situation where someone was not really listening to you. How did that make you feel?
- What can this activity tell us about communication?

"Now What" Questions
- What problems can occur when we don't communicate clearly?
- How can we improve our communication with others?

BLOW HARD

TOPIC AREA: Anger Management, Conflict Resolution, Violence

CONCEPT: Most violence is preceded by someone getting mad. Therefore if we want to reduce the incidents of violence, it would be productive to deal with one of violence's underlying factors which is anger management. Many of our children and youth today do not know how to handle their anger so they react by striking out at the offending person. If we can show them how ineffective this reaction is in really solving their problems, hopefully violence will not be their first and only solution. Blowing up or acting out do not solve problems. These reactions may create a temporary feeling of relief, but long term solutions to conflicts can only be worked out through communication and understanding.

METHOD: Classroom demonstration

TIME ESTIMATE: 5 minutes plus discussion time

MATERIALS NEEDED:
• 3 pieces of 8½ x 11 clear acetate or overhead transparency material
• 1 ping pong ball
• Clear tape

ACTIVITY: Before the demonstration begins, you will need to prepare three funnels. Take the three pieces of clear plastic and roll each of them into a funnel. The bottom opening should be about a quarter of an inch in

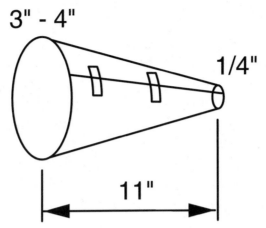

Fig. 1

diameter and the top opening should be about 3½ to 4 inches across. Use the clear tape to hold the sheets in the funnel shape. (See figure 1) By using a clear material, the class will be able to watch the progress of the participants.

To begin the demonstration, invite three participants to the front of the room. Give each of them one of the funnels that you created. Then hand the ping pong ball to the first person and ask them to place it inside of the funnel. Now challenge them to hold the funnel high and blow into the bottom, trying to blow the ping pong ball out of the funnel. (See figure 2) Once they have made their attempt, repeat the process with the other two participants.

It is impossible to blow the ping pong ball out of the funnel. The reason is that as soon as the ball is pushed up in the funnel, air then passes around the edge of the ball. No matter how hard you blow, your efforts will only cause the ball to jump up and down, never all the way

out. This is a perfect illustration of what happens when someone gets mad and blows up. Just as the ball drops back into place after you give it a hard blow, when you get mad there is a lot of effort expended but the problem remains. Getting mad doesn't solve anything.

Fig. 2

DISCUSSION IDEAS:

"What" Questions
- How much success did they have?
- How hard were they trying?
- If we let them try longer, would they have any better success?

"So What" Questions
- Did blowing harder make a difference in getting the ball out of the funnel?
- How can we relate this demonstration to solving a problem by getting mad?
- After you get mad, is the problem solved? Why or why not?
- How easy is it to solve problems when people are angry?

- How does anger affect the person who is angry? The other person?
- Can anger lead to violence? Why or why not?
- What must be done to solve a problem between two people?

"Now What" Questions
- What are some positive ways to express your anger?
- What are some positive ways to keep your anger under control?
- How can you solve a conflict without resorting to anger?

TNT IDEA: Use a magic marker to color the ping pong ball to make it stand out.

BLUE OR PINK?

TOPIC AREA: School to Careers, Stereotyping

CONCEPT: Stereotyping based on gender is a common behavior exhibited in our society today. The situation has improved somewhat in recent years, but we still see advertising, career choices, advancement opportunities, expectations regarding behavior and other areas that reveal a bias regarding gender in our society. These attitudes begin at a very young age. We dress boys in blue and girls in pink to reveal their gender. Just try to dress a little boy in a pink outfit and see the reactions. We encourage boys to play with trucks and girls to play with dolls because society believes that this is what they will enjoy. Beginning with very basic assumptions, gender bias or expectations begin to be created. Our beliefs regarding what boys and girls should be like and what they should do are reinforced throughout many areas of our society.

METHOD: Classroom activity

TIME ESTIMATE: 10 minutes plus discussion time

MATERIALS NEEDED:
- 1 story per person (make copies of those provided)
- 1 piece of paper per pair
- 1 pen or pencil per pair

ACTIVITY: Have everyone get a partner. Give each pair a piece of paper and a writing utensil. Pass out a story to each person. Both partners receive the same story. Before distributing the stories, fill in the age of Michael and Mia with an age that is around the ages of the group you are working with. Give one half of the group the story about Michael and the other half the story about Mia. Explain that they are to read the story and then answer the questions at the bottom. After the partners have answered the questions together, have them share their results with the entire group. For comparison purposes, list the responses on the board for both Michael and Mia.

Michael's Story: Michael is ____ years old. He likes sports a lot and spends a lot of his time watching and participating. He is also a good student in school and is well liked by everyone. Michael has two older brothers, a younger sister and a dog. He has a number of hobbies that keep him busy. Michael is looking forward to someday getting a good job. He is an innovative thinker, can create things with his hands, works well with people, wants to enjoy his chosen career and is willing to live anywhere in the country.

- Name three sports you think Michael plays.
- List three hobbies you think Michael has.
- Name three birthday gifts you think Michael would like to receive.
- List three jobs you think Michael be likely to have.

Mia's Story: Mia is ____ years old. She likes sports a lot and spends a lot of her time watching and participating. She is also a good student in school and is well liked by everyone. Mia has two older brothers, a younger sister and a dog. She has a number of hobbies that keep her busy. Mia is looking forward to someday getting a good job. She is an innovative thinker, can create things with her hands, works well with people, wants to enjoy her chosen career and is willing to live anywhere in the country.

- Name three sports you think Mia plays.
- List three hobbies you think Mia has.
- Name three birthday gifts you think Mia would like to receive.
- List three jobs you think Mia would be likely to have.

VARIATION: Have some pairs be male, some be female and some be mixed. At the end of the activity see if there are any differences between how the pairs answered the questions.

DISCUSSION IDEAS:

"What" Questions
- Did you and your partner have a hard time agreeing on your answers?
- How did your answers compare with those who had the same story as you did?
- How did your answers compare with those who had a different story than you did?

"So What" Questions
- Are the answers different for Michael and Mia?
- Do the answers reflect the fact that Michael is a boy and Mia is a girl?
- Do we make assumptions about people based on their gender? Is this fair?
- Why do we think that certain things are for boys and certain things are for girls? Is this type of thinking right or wrong? Explain.
- How does the workplace reflect society's thinking about gender?

- What are some jobs where we find more males than females? More females than males? What is it about these jobs that make them gender oriented?
- List jobs that people think of as jobs for men. Can women do any or all of these jobs?
- List jobs that people think of as jobs for women. Can men do any or all of these jobs?
- How does gender stereotyping influence what we like and what we do?
- How do advertisers and stores use gender to sell their products?

"Now What" Questions
- Why is gender stereotyping harmful to our society?
- What information should we use about a person when evaluating what they like or what they are capable of doing?
- What role should gender have in deciding what we like and what we become?

TNT IDEA: For groups that do not write well, divide the group into two teams. Assign one team Michael and the other team Mia. Have one person record the responses for each team on a piece of large tablet paper. When finished, compare the answers from each team. Be sure the teams can't hear each discussing the answers or the element of surprise will disappear.

BRIDGES

TOPIC AREA: Problem Solving

CONCEPT: Life is not a true/false test; it is all essay! Once we leave the classroom there are continually problems to solve that don't necessarily have one correct answer. It takes critical thinking and perseverance to figure out a workable solution. The workplace is looking for people who have the initiative to think for themselves and find solutions to complex problems. Challenging our children and youth to solve problems will help them build the critical thinking skills they will need to succeed in today's changing society.

METHOD: Classroom activity

TIME ESTIMATE: 30 minutes

MATERIALS NEEDED:
- 1 book per person (The books should be at least ½ inch thick)
- 2 pieces of 8½ by 11 paper per person
- 2 toothpicks per person
- 2 inches of masking tape per person
- 25 pennies per person
- A ruler

ACTIVITY: Have each person sit across from another person. Give each pair two books, fifty pennies and two pieces of 8½ by 11 paper. Have them place the books, lying flat, between them. The books must be ten inches

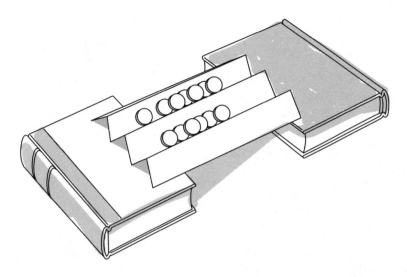

apart from each other. Use a ruler to be sure that they are placed exactly ten inches apart.

Here is the challenge. Each person must create a bridge out of the piece of paper that spans the distance between the two books. They may fold the paper however they like, but it may not touch the ground and must rest on top of the books. When they have completed their bridge, have them see how many pennies it can support before the paper either touches the ground or any of the pennies fall off. The pair does not work as a team. Each person creates their own bridge. The reason for sitting in pairs is simply to reduce the number of books and pennies needed for the activity. Record how many pennies each person's bridge was able to hold.

For round two give each person a new piece of paper, two toothpicks and two inches of masking tape. Explain that the challenge is the same except that this time they may use the additional materials to strengthen their bridge. The only rule is that they may not use the tape to attach the ends of the paper to the books. If they use all fifty pennies and their bridge is still standing, you have the option of letting them borrow pennies from another group or stating that fifty will be the top number they are shooting for. Record how many pennies each person's bridge was able to hold.

DISCUSSION IDEAS:

"What" Questions
- How many pennies did your bridge hold in round one? In round two?
- What building technique did you use in round one? In round two?
- What building technique worked best for you?
- If you were able to repeat this activity, what would you do differently?

"So What" Questions
- How did you decide on the kind of bridge you wanted to build in round one?
- What changes were you able to make in round two with the addition of new materials?
- How many ideas did you have before you began to work?
- Did you stick with your original idea or did you make changes?
- If you made changes were they beneficial?
- Should we use the first idea we think of when trying to solve a problem? Why or why not?
- Did you look at what other people were doing to get ideas? Would that be considered cheating? (Mention that this would not be cheating. You did not tell them they couldn't.)

- How does creative thinking help us find a solution to a problem?
- Should we give up if our first idea doesn't work? Why or why not?

"Now What" Questions
- Why should we continue to try even when our first idea doesn't work?
- How could asking for help from others improve our decision making ability?

BULL'S-EYE

TOPIC AREA: Communication, Working Together

CONCEPT: Clear communication is the foundation of our society. This is true whether we are talking about a relationship between two people or when working on a group project. Vague comments such as, "Good job!" are not helpful feedback. To really be helpful, a comment should be specific such as, "That was a great idea to use the computer to send out those letters so quickly!" Both statements could make the person feel better, but the second statement gives them specific feedback that can help them evaluate what to do in future situations. Being specific is not always easy, but the benefits in improved future behavior certainly outweigh the effort.

One place I have found this activity to be extremely useful is when teaching "I statements" or "I messages". A number of curriculum use this technique to help kids express their feelings in a positive manner. This activity can be used to reinforce the point that when making an "I statement or message" you need to be specific.

METHOD: Classroom activity

TIME ESTIMATE: 15 minutes plus discussion time

MATERIALS NEEDED:
- 4 pieces of 8½ by 11 inch paper per team of 4 or 5 people
- 1 large paper grocery bag or bucket per team
- Masking tape

ACTIVITY: Divide your group into teams of four to five people. Give each team a paper sack and four pieces of paper. Place a piece of masking tape down on the floor to make the starting line. Set the bag up about six feet away from the starting line. Have the teams line up single file behind the starting line. Give the first person in each line the four pieces of paper. Have them crumple the papers up so they make four balls.

The last person in each line goes out to stand by the paper bag and be the helper. This person serves as the instruction giver, retriever and, if necessary, to hold the bag open. They may not physically assist the thrower. The first person turns backwards so they are facing away from the paper bag. They must now toss the four

pieces of paper over their shoulder, one at a time, trying to get them to land in the bag. They may not turn around nor talk once they begin their set of four throws. The helper who is standing by the paper bag will be their eyes. After each throw the helper will describe where the paper ball landed and how to change the thrower's aim for the next throw. No one else on the team may give suggestions or help to the thrower. After the thrower takes their four tosses they take the place of the helper. The helper retrieves the paper balls, takes them back to the team and goes to the end of the line. The second person in line rotates up and now becomes the thrower. Go through the entire line one time. The team receives ten points for each paper ball that makes it into the bag.

DISCUSSION IDEAS:

"What" Questions
- How many pieces of paper did your team get into the bag?
- How hard was it for you to get them in the bag?
- What made giving instructions difficult?
- What technique for throwing did you find worked best?
- What technique for giving instructions did you find worked best?
- If you were to try this again, what would you do differently?

"So What" Questions
- What can this activity tell us about communication?
- How specific were the instructions that the helper gave to you?

- What would have happened if your helper just said "Nice job, but try a little harder."
- Were the instructions clear enough that they were helpful?
- How could the instructions have been more helpful?
- Did you learn from your helper how to give good (or bad) instructions?
- Why is communication important when working in a group?
- How does communication affect how much a group can achieve?

"Now What" Questions

- What do we have to do to communicate clearly?
- How does being specific help us to communicate better?
- How does specific feedback help us to work together?

COLOR BLIND

TOPIC AREA: Diversity, Stereotyping

CONCEPT: Our society seems to be fixated on the color of a person's skin. We try to pass laws relating to skin color, we make judgments about people based on skin color, we create television shows about people of color and we base some of what we think we know about people based on their skin color. Using skin color as a basis for making decisions about other people leads us down a path of misinformation and errors in judgment. Our country is made up of a collection of different types of people who bring a wide variety of backgrounds to the table. It is this very diversity of backgrounds that makes our society able to achieve the successes that we have. Skin color is not the only stereotype that we base our judgments of other people on, but it is one of the most obvious and widespread.

METHOD: Classroom demonstration

TIME ESTIMATE: 5 minutes plus discussion time

MATERIALS NEEDED:
- 4 glasses
- Milk
- A spoon
- Hershey's chocolate syrup

ACTIVITY: Pour about half a glass of milk into each of the four glasses. Place them on a table in the front of the room. Explain that today you are going to talk about skin color and people. Skin color varies from one person to another and from one group of people to another. Now take a small amount of chocolate syrup and stir it into the second glass. Use only enough syrup so it turns a very light brown. Explain that the substance in our bodies that determines our skin color is called melanin. The more melanin a person has, the darker their skin color will be. Melanin protects the skin from the harmful rays of the sun. Therefore people whose ancestors originally lived in climates that had a lot of sun, such as around the equator, produced more melanin and had darker skin. Those people whose ancestors lived in areas farther away from the sun, such as Greenland, needed less protection from the sun and therefore had less melanin in their skin which resulted in lighter colored skin. Add chocolate syrup to the remaining two glasses of milk. Add varying amounts so that each glass of milk becomes increasingly darker.

DISCUSSION IDEAS:

"What" Questions
- How many people do you know that have skin color that matches the white of glass number one?
- We call some people "white" and other people "black" are they really those colors?
- What happened as we added the chocolate syrup to the milk?
- As we added chocolate syrup, did the milk change into something else?

"So What" Questions
- How can we relate this activity to the color of people's skin?

- How does a person's outward appearance impact what we think about them?
- Does the color of a person's skin determine how a person acts? Why or why not?
- When a person tans, does it make them a different person? Why not?
- What can we figure out about a person based on the color of their skin?
- What can we figure out about a person based on other outward differences such a height, hair color or gender?
- What does it mean to stereotype a person?
- How do we stereotype people based on their skin color?
- Is stereotyping an accurate way to judge people?

"Now What" Questions
- What role should outward appearances play in how we think about others?
- What are some ways to help us not judge others based on how they look?

CROSSING THE LINE

TOPIC AREA: Decision Making

Concept: I saw a church sign that said "Too often trouble starts out as fun!" As we look at the trouble our kids can get into, we can see how true this statement is. We want them to have fun and experience life to its fullest. What we don't want is their quest for fun to cross over the line and become illegal, dangerous or risky. Kids don't always plan to get into trouble, sometimes it just happens. Take skiing for example. You can have a lot of fun on the slopes, but what about the area that is off limits to skiers? It looks so inviting. So you just go for it! Bad decision. Sure it may look like fun, but there was a reason for it to be marked off limits. Now there may be consequences such as legal problems or injuries to deal with. Other examples could include how a trip to the mall results in shoplifting or joking around leads to a fist fight. We don't want to discourage our kids from having fun, but we do want them to know that their decisions have consequences. Children and youth should be aware of the problems associated with various behaviors and don't get so close to the line that divides fun and trouble that they can easily cross over it. The message needs to be "Have fun but don't cross the line".

METHOD: Classroom activity

TIME ESTIMATE: 8 minutes plus discussion time

MATERIALS NEEDED:
- A penny for each team of two

- A ruler for each team of two
- A piece of paper for each team of two
- A pen or a pencil for each team of two
- A desk or a table space for each team of two (More than one team can be seated at a table)

ACTIVITY: Have everyone get a partner and have them stand or sit opposite each other at a desk or table. The distance from one side of the desk or table to the other should be at least eighteen inches. Give each pair a penny. The object is to use your finger to flick or fling the penny so it slides across the top of the table and see how close you can come to the opposite edge without going off of the table. The purpose of having a partner on the opposite side of the table is simply to allow the penny to be shot back and forth and to help retrieve the penny if it goes over the edge. Give the participants about three minutes to practice sliding their penny across the table top. This will give them a chance to get a feel for how the penny slides and which propulsion method works best for them.

After allowing them time to practice explain that they will have five tries to get as close to the opposite edge of the table as possible. One person will take a turn and then the other person will take a turn until each person has had their five tries. They will use a ruler to measure each try Have them measure from the edge of the table they are shooting towards to the closest edge of the penny. After each of the five attempts, have them record the distance. The winner will be the person who gets the closest to the edge without falling off of the table. If they get it to stop with part of the penny hanging over the edge without falling off, they measure how much of the penny is hanging over. They will only report out their closest distance, not all five. Once everyone has taken their five tries, have them report out their best effort.

DISCUSSION IDEAS:

"What" Questions
- What methods did you experiment with during the practice rounds to shoot the penny?
- What method worked best for you to shoot the penny?
- How close did you come to the edge of the table?
- How many times did you shoot the penny off the table?

"So What" Questions
- How well could you control where the penny would stop?
- How much control did you have over the penny once it started moving?
- Do we always have control over exactly what happens in our lives?
- What areas in our lives do we control by the decisions we make?
- How are our actions affected by the decisions we make?
- How can our decisions get us into trouble?
- How can our decisions keep us out of trouble?
- It was hard to stop the penny right next to the edge. How hard is it to make a good decision when you are in the middle of having fun?
- How easy is it for fun to cross the line and turn into trouble?
- Describe situations where fun crosses the line and turns into trouble.

- What role do consequences play in decision making?
- Who pays the consequences for a person's good decisions? Poor decisions?

"Now What" Questions
- How can we keep from crossing the line from fun to trouble?
- How do our actions reflect the decisions we make?

TNT IDEA: If the measuring part is too time consuming, you can award points. An example of this would be, one point if the penny touches the edge, two points if part of the penny hangs over the edge and minus three points if the penny goes off of the table.

DOWNHILL SLIDE

TOPIC AREA: Alcohol and Other Addicting Drugs

CONCEPT: Youth always feel they are immortal and that nothing will ever happen to them. They believe that becoming addicted is something that happens to winos on skid row and people who are down and out. However, the truth is that addiction can and does happen to all types of people. Addiction can affect people from all economic levels and from all types of social backgrounds. The addiction process has four steps which start with experimentation, then progress to regular use, daily preoccupation and finally dependency. In teens these steps can happen in as little as six to eighteen months due to the still-developing nature of their bodies. As the addiction continuum progresses through each step, the individual experiences a greater and greater loss of control. The addiction process takes over their life and the drug begins to exert more control over their lives with increasing consequences. This activity will take the participants through that loss of control.

METHOD: Classroom activity

TIME ESTIMATE: 20 minutes plus discussion time

MATERIALS NEEDED:
- 12 small pieces (approximately 2½ x 4 inches) of paper per participant. You will need four different colors of paper.
- 1 writing utensil per participant

ACTIVITY: Before you begin the activity, cut twelve small pieces of paper per participant. You want to have four sets of three pieces of paper for each participant. For each set use a different color of paper. Keep track of which color of paper you assign to each of the four categories. This will make it easier for you to refer to these four categories when you are reading the scenarios and asking them to choose various papers to discard. The four categories that will be used are people who are special to them, things or possessions, activities, or personal attributes and abilities.

Begin by giving each participant twelve pieces of paper and a writing utensil. Distribute the papers so each participant receives four different sets of three pieces of colored paper. For example each person would receive three blue pieces of paper, three green pieces of paper, three white pieces of paper and three yellow pieces of paper.

Instruct each person to write the names of three separate people who they like a lot on three separate pieces of paper. You should tell them which color to use so that everyone uses the same color for this step. On three pieces of another color of paper (once again you choose the color so that everyone uses the same color) write three things or possessions that they regard as special. On three pieces of the same color of paper write three different activities in which they enjoy participating. On the last three pieces of colored of paper write three personal attributes, abilities, talents or characteristics about themselves that they feel good about. Have each person pair up with a partner.

Explain the four steps of alcohol addiction (see concept) and that with each stage there is a greater and greater loss of control over their lives. You will now read to them a number of different scenarios. After each scenario, give them directions regarding the papers that they just filled out.

Scenario one: You have been invited to a party. You come home late after curfew, smelling of alcohol. Your parents are waiting up for you. You're in big trouble! One of your possessions is taken away as punishment. You must choose which one. Choose one of your possession papers and tear it up.

Give the participants 20 seconds to choose which possession to tear up.

Scenario two: After a Friday night football game you and a friend go to a mutual friend's house. His/her parents are not home and there is beer available. You decide to drink quite a bit. The next morning you have a hangover and are not able to participate in one of your favorite activities. Tear up one activity papers and one personal attribute papers.

Give the participants 15 seconds to choose which activity and personal attribute to tear up.

Scenario three: Drinking has become one of your favorite things to do. You are now looking forward to drinking every weekend. You feel you can handle it - it's not a problem. Tear up one person paper and one personal attribute paper.

Give participants 10 seconds to choose which person and personal attribute to tear up.

Scenario four: You now find yourself drinking daily with serious consequences: suspended from school, stealing money, fighting with your parents. Tear up one person paper and one personal attribute paper.

Give participants 10 seconds to choose which person and personal attribute to tear up.

Scenario five: On your way home from a weekend of partying, you are picked up for a DUI. Tear up one possession square and one activity square.

Give the participants 5 seconds to choose which squares to tear up.

Scenario six: You are now totally at the mercy of your addition. Your life is out of control due to your alcohol use.

Ask the participants to hold the remaining three pieces of paper in their hand like they would hold a hand of playing cards. Have the participants turn and face their partner with their papers held so that their partner can't read what is written on the pieces of paper. Have each partner reach across and at random choose two pieces of paper from the other person's hand and tear them up. Each person will now be left with just one piece of paper.

DISCUSSION IDEAS:

"What" Questions
- How hard was it to choose three people who you like a lot?

- How hard was it to choose three possession to write down?
- How hard was it to choose three activities to write down?
- How hard was it to choose three personal attributes to write down?

"So What" Questions
- From which of the four categories was it most difficult to choose which square to tear up? Why?
- How did you feel as your pieces of paper were being torn up?
- How did the shortening of time you had to choose which cards to tear up impact your decision?
- How was it different when someone else chose the papers to tear up instead of you?
- How does this activity relate to a person who is going through the four stages of addiction?
- How does this activity show the loss of control an addicted person experiences?
- How does this activity show the consequences of addiction?

"Now What" Questions
- What can we do to avoid becoming addicted?
- If we know someone who is becoming or is already addicted, how can we best help them?

Adapted from an activity given to me by Tammi Reynolds from Bloomington, Illinois, with credit also to Linda Kolaya and Barbara Grimes-Smith. Thanks, Tammi.

DUELING CARDS

TOPIC AREA: Respect, School to Careers

CONCEPT: No matter how nurturing or friendly a workplace is, there will still be a hierarchy of authority. Students need to recognize that working within the structure of an organization is a skill they will need to master. In most cases, young workers will be amazed at how much freedom of expression and latitude they are actually given in how to complete assignments. However, part of that freedom depends upon them acknowledging the authority of the people over them. Respect plays a major role in how we treat others and how we treat others may determine our success in the workplace. This exercise will give students some exposure to workplace hierarchy.

METHOD: Classroom activity

TIME NEEDED: 7 minutes plus discussion time.

MATERIALS NEEDED:
- 1 playing card from a regular deck of cards for each participant (Do not use the Joker)
- 1 piece of paper per participant
- 1 pen or pencil per participant

ACTIVITY: Pass out a playing card, a piece of paper and a writing utensil to each participant. After they look at their card, caution them to keep the front of their card hidden from the other participants. Distribute all of the cards from one suit first, starting with the Ace and working your way down. For example, if you have only nine participants you would only distribute hearts. If you had up to twenty-six participants, you would only distribute hearts and spades. If you have to eliminate cards, eliminate the lower numbered cards first. Each card represents a position that you would find within a large company. Write on the board or on an overhead the relative positions that each card represents. The card representations are: Ace = Chairman of the Board, King = President, Queen = Vice-President, Jack = Director, 10 = Manager, 9 = Accountant, 8 - Supervisor, 7 - Office Assistant, 6 = Line Supervisor, 5 = Line Worker, 4 = Delivery Driver, 3 = Mail Room Worker, 2 = Custodian.

Once everyone has a card, have them pair up with a partner. Have each person look at the board to see what job title their card represents. You will then count to three. At the count of three, both people tell their job to their partner and show their card. Whoever has the card representing the higher position is the winner of the round. If both cards are the same value, then red beats out black due to seniority in the organization. If both cards are the same color and value then no one receives any points. The person with the winning card receives ten points. Have each person keep track of their own score. At the conclusion of each round, everyone must switch cards with their partner and then find a new partner. (Do not let them partner with the same person again throughout the rest of the activity, unless your group is small.) Once again, have them look at the board to see what position their new cards represents. Count to three again and have them reveal their positions. Repeat this same sequence for about seven rounds. Then have the participants report out their scores to the group.

VARIATION: If you want to more closely represent the workplace, you may distribute more lower numbered cards and fewer higher numbered cards.

DISCUSSION IDEAS:

"What" Questions
• How many points did you score?
• What was the highest position you had?
• What was the lowest position you had?
• How did you feel when you were holding a high card? A low card?

"So What" Questions
• What do the words authority, power and prestige mean in the workplace?
• How can you tell when a person has authority, power and prestige in the workplace?
• How would a person with a lower position on the company organizational chart show respect to someone at a higher level? Show a lack of respect?
• What would happen to someone who showed a lack of respect to those in a position of authority over them?
• Should a person with authority over others show respect to those who are below them on the company organizational chart? Why or why not?
• Should we automatically respect those who have authority over us?
• How is respect gained in the workplace? How is it lost?
• What part does respect for one another play in the success of a company?

"Now What" Questions
* Why is it important to show respect in the workplace?
* What behaviors do we see in someone who is showing respect?

Thanks to Craig Rasmussen from Ephraim, Utah for the concept of this activity!

END OF THE RAINBOW

TOPIC AREA: Goal Setting, Responsibility, School to Careers

CONCEPT: Some things are worth working for. The rewards of education can be measured in cold hard cash. According to national statistics, a person who does not complete high school can expect to earn $19,700 per year. If a person earns a high school diploma, they will earn an average of $26,000 per year. If that same person completes two years of education after high school, they can expect to receive $31,700 per year. This could be an associate's degree or training at a technical school. Upon receiving a college degree, the compensation rises to $40,100 per year and a master's degree will return an average yearly income of $50,000. These figures were taken from the Federal Bureau of Labor Statistics and represent median average earnings in 1997 dollars. You will need to make your students aware of these statistics before conducting the activity.

The moral of this story is that the more education a person receives, the higher their average salary will likely be. The question now becomes, what are you willing to work towards? Will you put in the effort to improve your chance of earning a good income by setting high goals? Or will you settle for a lesser salary because the effort seems to be too much? These decisions are up to you. No one else can decide for you. It is your responsibility and yours alone.

METHOD: Classroom activity

TIME ESTIMATE: 20 minutes plus discussion time

MATERIALS NEEDED:
- 3 grocery bags per team of five
- 3 pieces of 8½ x 11 paper per team of five
- Masking tape
- 1 pair of scissors
- Magic marker

ACTIVITY: Before the activity begins, cut the tops off of three grocery bags leaving the bag about six inches tall. Also crumple up three pieces of paper into balls for each team of five. Label one bag for each team "High School". Label one bag for each team "Additional Schooling". Label the third bag "College Degree".

To begin the activity, divide your group into teams of five. Give each team three cut down grocery bags and three pieces of crumpled up paper balls. Place a piece of masking tape down on the floor to indicate a starting line. Place three grocery bags in front of each team at varying distances from the starting line. The first bag, labeled "High School", should be about five feet away, the second bag, labeled "Additional Schooling", about seven feet away and the third bag, labeled "College Degree", about ten feet away. You can vary these distances depending upon the abilities of your students.
Explain to the teams that each person on their team will toss the three pieces of paper one at a time and try to have them land in one of the three bags. Each bag will be worth a different point total. If you land a paper ball in the closest bag, it will be worth 100 points. If you land a paper ball in the second bag, it will be worth 500 points. If you land a paper ball in the third bag it will be worth 2000 points. The thrower can aim for a different

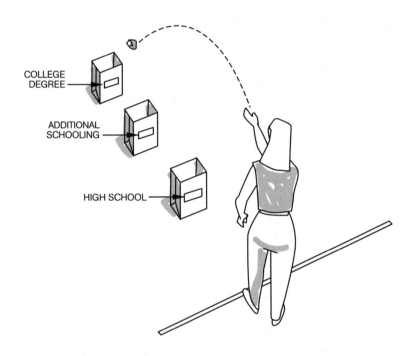

bag on each of their three throws or they may try for the same bag each time. After the first thrower has taken their three throws, have them go up and stand by the bags to retrieve the paper balls for the next person. Rotate the retrieving person with each new thrower. Have the teams go through a practice round before starting to keep score. Repeat with a second scoring round to see if they improve or make different choices as to which bags to aim for. Have the team scores reported out to the group after each of the two scoring rounds.

DISCUSSION IDEAS:

"What" Questions
- What was your total team score in round one? In round two?

- How did your scores compare with the scores of the other teams?
- How did you determine which bags to aim for?
- Did your strategy change during the activity? If so, how?

"So What" Questions
- Why were the bags worth more points as the distance increased?
- With practice do you think that you could improve your personal score?
- Would you be willing to work hard for something that you wanted? Why or why not?
- Getting more education is not always easy, but what is the probable result in terms of income?
- What are some of the barriers that a person encounters when trying to get an education?
- What are some of the ways that those same barriers can be overcome?
- What role can others play in helping you achieve your education goals?
- Is money a measure of success in our society? Explain.
- What other criteria could we use to measure success?
- What problems arise in some people's lives when they lack an adequate amount of money?

"Now What" Questions
- What behaviors would we see in a person who is interested in getting a good education? Not interested?
- Whose responsibility is it for you to achieve a good education?
- What can a high level of education help you achieve?

FINGER TRAP

TOPIC AREA: Decision Making, Peer Pressure

CONCEPT: Many decisions are influenced by peer pressure. The greater the pressure, the harder it is to resist. Usually pressure becomes harder to resist the longer period of time over which it is applied. For example, if a young person goes to a party and when they walk in the door they see alcohol, it is easier at that point to turn around and walk out than it is to make the decision to leave later. Risky situations can include parties where alcohol is present, cheating in school, kids talking about vandalism or shoplifting, etc. The longer you stay in a risky situation, the more likely it is that you will make an unwise decision. The solution to the problem of peer pressure is to make your decision at the first sign of trouble rather than waiting around to see what happens. Peer pressure can't affect you if you are no longer in the risky situation.

METHOD: Classroom activity

TIME ESTIMATE: 6 minutes plus discussion time

MATERIALS NEEDED: None

ACTIVITY: Divide your group into teams of three. If you can't divide into teams of three, have one or more teams consist of four people. In round number one, have each person on the team hold their left hand out to their left side with the palm facing up. The palm should be

Fig. 1

held as flat or as wide open as possible at about waist level. Now have each person make a fist with their right hand with just their index finger pointing out. Place the index finger of their right hand into the center of the palm of the person on their right. The finger should be placed so it forms a right angle with the palm. (See figure 1) Just the tip of the pointing index finger should be touching the palm. All three members of the team are now touching. This will result in them forming a circle. (See figure 2)

Explain that you are going to count to three. On the number three, each person tries to remove there finger

Fig. 2

from the palm of the person on their right. At the same time, the person on the right is trying to close their hands fast enough to capture the other person's finger before they can get away. You receive 50 points for an escape and 50 points for a capture. If a player was to successfully remove his or her finger from the palm and at the same time successfully capture another person's finger they could receive a total of 100 points for that round. Repeat this at least three times. Vary the rate that you count to three so the players can't time your pattern and get a jump. If someone does go early, they are charged a penalty of minus 50 points.

For round number two have each person once again hold their left hand at waist level. This time the hand should be in a "U" shape with the thumb and index finger towards the ceiling and the little finger towards the floor. Their thumb and fingers should be about two inches apart. Have them again form a fist with their right hand with their index finger pointing out. They will then put their index finger into the "U" shaped hand of the person on their right. They will put the index finger down into the "U" shaped hand as far as their first knuckle. This will make the first knuckle even with the bottom of the index finger of the "U" shaped hand. (See figure 3) The rest of the procedure is the same as in round number one.

Fig. 3

For round number three, make only one small change from round number two. This time the finger is placed further down into the "U" shaped hand of the person on

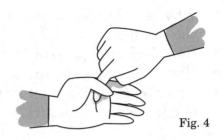

Fig. 4

their right. For this round they must put their finger in down to their second knuckle. This will place their second knuckle even with the bottom of the index finger of the "U" shaped hand. (See figure 4)

Have each person keep track of their own score throughout the activity. If you would like, you can change groups after each round so they don't compete against the same people each time. What you will see is that as the finger is placed further down into the hand next to them, the harder it becomes to escape.

DISCUSSION IDEAS:

"What" Questions
- What was your score?
- How hard was it to escape in round one? Round two? Round three?
- How hard was it to capture the index finger in round one? Round two? Round three?
- What made the difference in each of the rounds?

"So What" Questions
- Why was it harder to escape in rounds two and three?
- What does the phrase "peer pressure" mean?
- Give some examples of how peer pressure is applied.

- Why is it harder to resist peer pressure the longer you are faced with it?
- How does peer pressure wear you down?
- How does peer pressure affect your decisions?
- Describe some risky situations where leaving would eliminate peer pressure.

"Now What" Questions
- What should you do when you get into a risky situation?
- Why would it be easier to make a decision to leave a risky situation as soon as you enter it instead of after you have been there for a while?

TNT IDEA: Instead of doing the activity in groups of three, have everyone in one big circle.

This activity was adapted from a suggestion by Floyd Asonwha from Kenosha, Wisconsin. Thanks Floyd!

FIRE BRIGADE

TOPIC AREA: Alcohol, Drugs

CONCEPT: When a person uses any kind of a drug, it has an effect on the body. When alcohol or another depressant-type drug is used, the body will respond by slowing down its reaction time. When your reaction time is impaired in such a manner, it becomes more difficult for you to complete certain tasks. This is especially true for tasks which require a rapid response time or quick thinking. Examples of these tasks could be found while you are driving or riding a bike, during school, while participating in extra-curricular activities or at the workplace.

METHOD: Classroom activity

TIME ESTIMATE: 15 minutes plus discussion time

MATERIALS NEEDED:
- 2 paper cups per team of four or five
- 8 pennies per team
- 1 plastic spoon per person (easily acquired for free just by asking at many fast food outlets or from the school cafeteria)
- A watch with a second hand

ACTIVITY: Divide your group into teams of four or five. Have each team line up in a straight line, with the people standing shoulder to shoulder. Place one paper cup on the floor or on a chair in front of the team and one

paper cup at the back of the line on the floor or a chair. Put eight pennies in the cup that is at the front of the line. Give each team member a plastic spoon. Explain that the object is to move the pennies from the cup in the front of the line to the cup at the rear of the line as fast as you can. The pennies must be moved down the line one at a time. A second penny may not be started until the first one has been dropped into the end cup. The penny must be passed from spoon to spoon. No one may touch the pennies with their hands and that includes the first and last person in the line. The first person may pick up the cup and tilt it to help get just one penny into their spoon. If a penny drops, it must be picked up by the person who dropped it (they may use their hand to do so) and started again from the point where it was dropped. When the last person puts the penny into the cup at the end of the line, that person moves to the front of the line, uses their spoon to remove a penny from the cup and starts it down the line. When each team finishes, record their time.

Round two is done the same way with one significant change. The spoon must be held in the opposite hand. Therefore a right handed person must use their left hand and vice-versa. Once again record each team's time when they finish and compare times between rounds one and two.

VARIATION: If you want to make it more difficult, use marbles instead of pennies.

DISCUSSION IDEAS:

"What" Questions
- What was your team's time in the first round? The second round?
- How difficult was it to move the penny using your dominant hand? The opposite hand?
- How did you feel when using your opposite hand?

"So What" Questions
- How can this activity be compared to attempting tasks while impaired by alcohol or other drugs?
- List activities that would be harder for a person to accomplish if they were impaired.
- What problems would you have if you were impaired on the job?
- Are some people affected by drugs to a greater degree than others? Why or why not?
- Even if you don't use drugs, how can their use by others affect your life?
- How do impaired people affect others around them?

"Now What" Questions
- How can you avoid the problems of impairment?
- If one or your friends began using drugs, what should you do?

FIRST TIME

TOPIC AREA: Taking A Risk

CONCEPT: It's hard convincing kids to try something new. Many kids are so worried about being embarrassed or looking stupid that they would rather just not try something and miss out on the experience if there is a chance that people will laugh or think less of them. I've seen many kids standing on the sidelines watching others have fun instead of participating because "I'm just not good at that". Think of all of the things that you aren't good at the first time you try. Examples could be riding a bike, hitting a baseball, dancing, using a computer, cheerleading, swimming, etc. The list could be endless and would be different for different people. However, if your students never take a risk and try new things, then they will never have a chance to find out what they are really good at. If when learning to walk you quit the first time you fell down, we wouldn't have very many people walking around today.

METHOD: Classroom activity

TIME ESTIMATE: 5 minutes plus discussion time

MATERIALS NEEDED:
- 1 piece of paper for each person
- 1 pen or pencil for each person
- 1 watch with a second hand

ACTIVITY: Give each person a piece of paper and a writing utensil. Explain that you are going to give them twenty seconds (adjust the time longer for younger kids) to see how many times they can write their first and last name. They can do cursive or printing. Their name must be legible. Complete one round and see what the scores are. Then repeat a second time to see if they can improve. Now give it a third round.

After the third round, announce that you would like for them to give it one more try. However, this time you want them to move the writing utensil to their other hand. Be prepared for a lot of moaning and groaning. Ignore the griping and have them give it a try. Check their results for legibility and quantity. Compare this round's results with the first three rounds.

Here are some sayings that you can put around the room to emphasize the fact that you can't grow until you try new things. Use some of them during the discussion time.

- "Behold the turtle; it makes progress only when it sticks its neck out." James Bryant Conant
- "Things may come to those who wait, but only the things left by those who hustle." Abraham Lincoln
- "Those who feel certain they will not succeed are seldom mistaken." Frances Osgood
- "Don't let life discourage you; everyone who got where he/she is had to begin where he/she was." Richard Evans
- "Unless you try to do something beyond what you have already mastered, you will never grow." Ronald E. Osborn
- "A great pleasure in life is doing what people say you cannot do." Walter Gagehot

- "Genius is one percent inspiration and ninety-nine percent perspiration." Thomas A. Edison
- "All things are difficult before they are easy." John Norley
- "One's mind, once stretched by a new idea, never regains its original dimensions." Oliver Wendell Holmes
- "The greatest calamity is not to have failed, but to have failed to try." Anonymous
- "Progress always involves risk; you can't steal second base and keep your foot on first." Frederick Wilcox
- "If you never reach, you're never going to grab what you're after." Anonymous
- "If you think you can, or if you think you can't...you're right!" Unknown

DISCUSSION IDEAS:

"What" Questions
- How many times did you write your name in the first round?
- Did you improve in round two? Round Three? By how much?
- How many times did you write your name when using the opposite hand?

"So What" Questions
- How did you feel when you were writing your name in the first three rounds?
- What was your first reaction when asked to move your pen or pencil to the other hand?
- How hard did you try in round four compared to the other rounds? Explain.
- In what situations in life do you think people feel the way you did in round four?

- Why is it hard for us to try something for the first time?
- Why is it harder for us to try something for the first time in front of other people?
- If we want to grow as a person, why do we have to try new things?
- Choose a quote from the list above and explain what you think it means.

"Now What" Questions
- How can we get better at something?
- How can we make trying something for the first time easier to do?
- How can we support others when they try something new?

FORE!

TOPIC AREA: Communication

CONCEPT: Clear communication is important in today's society. Time, effort and money are wasted when we don't clearly communicate our needs or instructions to others. This activity can be used to point out the necessity of giving instructions that are easy to understand and that the person receiving those instructions must also do their part to be sure they heard the instructions correctly.

METHOD: Classroom activity

TIME ESTIMATE: 15 minutes plus discussion time

MATERIALS NEEDED:
*   An 8½ x 11 piece of paper for each person
*   A pen or pencil for each person
*   A watch with a second hand on it

ACTIVITY: Give everyone a piece of paper and a writing utensil. Explain that they are going to create a nine hole golf course on their piece of paper. Give a time limit (two to four minutes) for them to design their course. They need to mark nine holes scattered around the paper and label them with numbers one through nine. Then go back and put in some sand traps, water hazards and trees. Place an "X" somewhere on the paper to show where the course will begin. Do not show your course to anyone else.

Now have everyone get a partner. Assign the roles of partner A and partner B. Partner A closes their eyes. After partner A has closed their eyes, partner B will bring out the golf course they have designed and place partner A's pen or pencil on the starting mark. Partner B will verbally give directions to partner A as to where they should move their pen or pencil to reach each of the nine designated holes. They must go through the course in numerical order. They must go around the sand traps, water hazards, etc. Partner A may not talk. The object is to get through as quickly as possible. When each person finishes the course, have them raise their hand and tell them how long it took. Have them record their time. Allow about four minutes or so for them to be guided through the course and then call time even if everyone has not finished. If someone has not finished when you call time, then have them record four minutes as their time. Now switch roles and have partner A guide partner B through the course that partner A has drawn. After both partners have completed these exercises, have them add their times together to get a total team time. Report these times out to the whole group.

Variation: If your kids don't relate very well with golf courses you can substitute something else. Some examples would be a skateboard park, motorcycle course or mountain bike trail. Instead of holes, designate nine check in points that they must reach in the correct order.

DISCUSSION IDEAS:

"What" Questions
- How hard was the course you designed compared to the one your partner designed?
- How did your team's time compare to the rest of the group?
- How easy was it to follow the instructions that you were given?
- Which role did you like better, giving or receiving the instructions?

"So What" Questions
- What does this activity have to do with communication?
- Would it have been easier if the person drawing could talk? Why or why not?
- If you don't understand something someone has said, who should you ask to help you clear it up?
- Describe a situation where unclear communication could be dangerous.
- How can poor communication cause someone to become angry?

- Whose role is more important, the person talking or the person listening? Why?
- Why is good communication important in a family? In a friendship? At the workplace?
- How can you be sure that someone has understood you correctly?
- How can you be sure that you heard someone correctly?

"Now What" Questions
- What steps can we take to communicate more clearly?

TNT IDEAS: Show an example of what you mean by a golf course to the group before they begin to design their own. Use blindfolds since some kids have a hard time keeping their eyes closed when they are the person drawing.

GROUP BENEFITS

TOPIC AREA: Diversity, Working Together

CONCEPT: No one individual knows everything. Some people might think and act like they do, but in reality everyone is experienced in different areas due to their background, heritage, interests and abilities. When we look at a community we will see a melting of those experiences reflected in the values of that community. Individuals influence those groups to which they belong and the those groups influence the communities as a whole. Each group may add something different. Without each group's contribution, communities and the workplace would lose the richness that comes with diversity. Working together to produce a thriving community, profitable product or a successful concept happens when we accept not just the contributions of one or two individuals but the thoughts and suggestions of many people. A group can improve their work through the use of synergy, while an individual must use more energy to get the same result.

METHOD: Classroom activity

TIME ESTIMATE: 12 minutes plus discussion time

MATERIALS NEEDED:
* A pen or pencil for each team of four
* A piece of paper for each team of four
* A watch with a second hand

ACTIVITY: Divide your group into teams of four and have them sit in a circle. Give each team a writing utensil and a piece of paper. Explain that you are going to give them a challenge. They will have sixty seconds to complete the challenge. The challenge will consist of trying to create the longest list of answers possible from the categories that you will give them. As each team creates their list, the paper they are using to write down their answers will be passed around the circle with each person adding one answer to the list when it is their turn. A team may not have any duplicate answers. There is no talking as the paper is passed around the circle. If one person can not think of an answer, they must write the word "skip" on the paper and then pass it to the next person. The paper continues around the circle with each person either adding a new word or the word skip each time it comes to them. Remember there is no talking during the sixty seconds. When time has expired, have each group report out their total number of answers, skips do not count. Then have each team read their list. Repeat this three times using a different category for each round. Since the first person to write will have the easiest time, have each round begin with a different person.

For rounds four and five, use the same process except that the group may talk during the sixty seconds. They may brainstorm and suggest answers to whomever has the piece of paper at the moment. Remember that the paper must still be passed from person to person with each individual writing down an answer before it is passed on to the next person. The "skip" rule may still be used but with the group helping no one will likely have a need for it.

SUGGESTIONS FOR CATEGORIES:
- Animals with four legs
- Major league baseball teams
- Breakfast cereals
- Television shows
- Countries from around the world
- States in America
- Sports
- Colors
- Foods served at fast food restaurants
- Musical instruments

DISCUSSION IDEAS:

"What" Questions
- How many answers did your team get in each of rounds one, two and three?
- How many answers did your team get in rounds four and five?
- How did these numbers compare to the other groups?
- What category did you find the easiest? The hardest?
- If you could choose a category that wasn't listed, what would it be?

"So What" Questions
- What can this activity teach us about working together?
- Did one person on your team always contribute the most?
- If your team only had two people, how well would the team have done?
- Why was your team able to create a longer list when you were allowed to talk?
- Why can't one person know everything?

- What role does a person's interests play in what they know?
- How does a person's background influence how they live?
- Does having people with various experiences help a community thrive?
- How does working together help make a problem easier to solve?

"Now What" Questions
- How can people from different backgrounds help make a community a better place to live?
- How can people from different backgrounds help solve a problem?

HAIR TRIGGER

TOPIC AREA: Anger Management, Violence

CONCEPT: Everyone gets angry. However, everyone doesn't get angry about the same things. For one person, someone calls them a name and they become upset while the same name calling doesn't even get a rise out of another person. Nor does everyone react in the same way when they get angry. Some people sulk, others yell, while some respond by lashing out at the offending party. These behaviors can escalate into violence. This activity gives you a chance to talk about what makes individuals angry and how they express that anger. You may then discuss different ways they could handle their anger in the future.

METHOD: Classroom activity or classroom demonstration

TIME ESTIMATE: Activity - 20 minutes, Demonstration - 10 minutes plus discussion time

MATERIALS NEEDED:
Activity
- 1 mousetrap for each team of four or five
- 1 piece of paper for each participant
- 1 pen or pencil for each participant
- Masking tape

Demonstration:
- One mousetrap
- 1 sheet of 8½ by 11 piece of paper
- 1 pen or pencil
- Masking tape

ACTIVITY: Divide your group into teams of four or five. Have each group brainstorm for about sixty seconds things that make people angry. Have each group share one item from their discussion. Give each person a piece of paper and a writing utensil. Have them write on the piece of paper one thing that can make a person angry. For example, one thing that can make someone angry is when people call them names. Then have them write down a time when this kind of thing could happen. For example, a time when someone could be called names is during lunch at school. When everyone finishes have them crumple their paper up into a ball.

Have the teams line up single file behind pieces of masking tape placed on the floor perpendicular to the single file line. The masking tape will serve as the line that they must stay behind when throwing. Give each team a mousetrap and have them place it on the floor three to five feet from the masking tape line. This distance can be adjusted according to the ability of your group. You don't want it to be so easy that everyone hits the trap or so hard that no one hits the trap. Set the mousetraps. The object will be to see if, one at a time, the participants can trigger the mousetrap by throwing their piece of paper underhand at the trap while standing behind the line. The underhand throw must travel in an arch, not a straight line. After the first person throws their piece of paper, have them go out and stand behind the trap to collect each throw. When everyone

has gone through one time, the first person can bring the papers back and distribute one to each team member. It doesn't matter if they get their own paper back or not. Go through the team twice so that each person has two throws. Reset the mousetrap after each time someone springs it. Think safety when having the traps reset and when people are retrieving the papers. For younger children, the teacher rather than a student is the one to reset the trap. Every time the trap is sprung the team receives ten points.

DEMONSTRATION: (This method takes less time and reduces the need for close supervision of the mousetraps.) As a group, brainstorm things that make people angry. Write these items down on a piece of paper. Choose five or six people from your group to come up front. Put masking tape down on the floor to indicate a starting line. Set the mousetraps and put them on the floor about three to five feet from the masking tape. This distance can be adjusted according to the ability of your group. You don't want it to be so easy that everyone hits the trap or so hard that no one hits the trap from the starting line. Crumple up the paper that you wrote the list. Each person will get one throw each. If the mousetrap is sprung, then it will have to be reset before the next person throws. The same piece of paper is retrieved and used for each person.

DISCUSSION IDEAS:

"What" Questions
- How easy was it for the people to hit the mousetrap?
- What methods did the team members use to help their aim?
- (Demonstration only) What method would you have tried if you were one of the team members?
- (Activity only) How many points did your team get?

"So What" Questions
- The paper ball triggered the trap. List some things that trigger people's anger.
- Does everyone get angry over the same things? Why or why not?
- Why do some things make us angry on certain occasions but not on others?
- Describe how you can tell when someone is angry?
- How does the body react when a person becomes angry?
- What are some behaviors that people exhibit when they become angry?
- What are some of the consequences to becoming

angry?
- How do people treat someone who is angry?
- What does anger do to our thinking process?

"Now What" Questions
- How can a person make it less likely that they will become angry?
- What are some negative ways we handle anger?
- What are some positive ways we handle anger?

HE SAID ... SHE SAID

TOPIC AREA: Respect, Violence

CONCEPT: Remember when your parents used to tell you, "If you don't have anything nice to say, don't say anything at all?" What we say has a definite impact on others. Another old saying goes, "Sticks and stones may break my bones but words will never harm me." This saying could not be further from the truth. Words can and do hurt people. Sometimes hurtful things are said out of anger or frustration. Other times they are part of a calculated plan to make someone feel bad. Gossip and rumors affect our children and teens just as much as they affect us. Schools and playgrounds are breeding places for such behavior to take place. The problem is once you say something, how do you take it back? Saying you're sorry doesn't ease the hurt that someone has felt as a result of your words. How do you stop a rumor? Once a rumor has been started, someone is sure to repeat it and even add to the story to make it sound even juicer. If we respect others then we will honor them through our words. The use of hurtful words does not show respect and can lead to violence. Most fights start with words being exchanged. The only way to be sure that your words do not harm others is to "think before you speak" (have you ever heard that one before?), because "unsaying" what you have already said is next to impossible.

METHOD: Classroom demonstration

TIME ESTIMATE: 5 minutes plus discussion time

MATERIALS NEEDED:
*   A trial size (usually less than 1 ounce) tube of toothpaste
*   A magic marker
*   An overhead projector
*   1 blank overhead transparency
*   1 plastic knife (easily acquired at a local fast food establishment)
*   A ruler
*   A watch with a second hand

ACTIVITY: Use a magic marker to draw a series of lines vertically on an overhead transparency. The lines should be dark and about one quarter of an inch wide and approximately 10 inches long. Make about eight lines on the overhead. To begin the demonstration, call one person up to the front of the room. Give them a small tube of toothpaste. Explain that the object is for the person to see how many of the lines they can cover with toothpaste. They are going for distance. They want to see how many inches of black lines they can cover with the toothpaste. The toothpaste must completely cover the line so none of it shows through. After you say begin, give them about fifteen to twenty seconds or until they run out of toothpaste to cover as much of the lines as they can. When time has expired, measure how many inches of the black magic marker line they were able to cover.

Now give the person a plastic table knife. Explain that they now have fifteen to twenty seconds to see how much of the toothpaste they can fit back into their toothpaste tube. The toothpaste must go back inside of the

tube. It may not sit on the top of the tube or remain on the knife. Have them start scraping the toothpaste from the end of one of the covered lines. Once again use the ruler to measure how much of the line they uncovered.

DISCUSSION IDEAS:

"What" Questions
- How many inches were covered with toothpaste?
- Did they have a hard time getting the toothpaste out of the tube?
- Did they roll up the tube or just squeeze it?
- How many inches of the black line were they able to successfully uncover and get back into the tube?
- Why couldn't they get more toothpaste back into the tube?

"So What" Questions
- If we compare words to toothpaste, how hard is it for us to take back something we said?
- Can words hurt other people's feelings? Explain.

- Once harsh or angry words have been spoken, what can we do to help the situation?
- How does anger affect the words we say?
- How can words lead to violence?
- How can we show respect to someone by the words we use?
- How do rumors start?
- Why do rumors and gossip spread so fast?
- If you hear a rumor, who is the best person to check with to see if it is true?
- Why would people say, "If you don't have anything nice to say, don't say anything at all?"

"Now What" Questions
- Since we know words can hurt others, what should we do before we speak?
- What should we do if we hurt someone else with our words?
- How can we help stop a rumor once it gets started even if we didn't start it?

HERE'S WHAT I SAW

TOPIC AREA: Conflict Resolution, Problem Solving

CONCEPT: "There are two sides to every story." How many times have you heard that statement? Well actually there are usually three sides to every story. Your side, their side and the cold, hard facts. It's not that we consciously lie when describing what took place in a certain event, but our beliefs and assumptions all color what we say. Each person is a collection of past experiences that we carry with us. We react to what we see using those experiences as a filter through which we interpret the facts. This is why people can see the same event and yet have different responses to the event. In solving a conflict we must be able to set aside the biases that we bring to the conflict and concentrate only on the event at hand. By not coloring the facts with our preconceived beliefs we can better understand what the real problem is rather than what we think it might be. The other part of this lesson is to put yourself in the other person's shoes and try to understand what they are seeing rather than just arguing that your views are the correct views. A conflict will never be resolved as long as both parties are only looking at their own side of the story.

METHOD: Classroom activity

TIME ESTIMATE: 15 minutes plus discussion time

MATERIALS NEEDED:

- A piece of paper that is black on one side and white on the other (One option would be to use a piece of black and a piece of white construction paper glued together)
- A copy of the story "On The Road" (Story is included below)

ACTIVITY: Before the activity prepare a piece of paper so that one side of it is black and the other side of it is white. The easiest way to do this is to use two pieces of construction paper, one white and one black, and glue them together. Keep the paper out of sight. Begin by bringing two students up to the front of the room. Have the two students face each other and close their eyes. Now bring the paper out and hold it between them at eye level with the black side facing one student and the white side facing the other student. Have them open their eyes. Ask each student, "What color do you see?" For effect, repeat the question when both of them give different answers. Then ask the class "Why are they giving different answers when they are both looking at the same piece of paper?" After taking comments, show the class that the paper is actually two colors.

Now read the following story. Explain that they should listen carefully because you will be asking for feedback.

On The Road

One afternoon a man and his family are driving slowly along a road enjoying the view when in the distance they see a boy lying in the grass off to the side of the asphalt. They could barely spot him because the weeds were so tall. Down in the ravine they can also see a bike laying down. As they get closer to the boy, they see him raise up slightly and cock his arm as if he is going to throw something. Sure enough, the boy lets loose with a rock thrown out into the street. As the car gets closer, they see him wind up and throw another rock directly at their car. The man speeds up to get away as quickly as possible, but the boy has time to throw one more rock which hits the side window and causes it to crack. The kids in the back seat scream and duck down as low as they can. The car continues to speed off. A couple of miles away, the man spots a police car. He stops and complains to the police officer that there is a crazy kid back on the side of the road hiding in the weeds throwing rocks at passing cars. He wants him arrested for breaking his car window and putting his kids in danger.

Stop reading at this point and ask, "Raise your hand if you agree that the driver has a right to want the police to deal with this boy?" Acknowledge, without comment, those that raise their hand.

Continue by saying, "Now here is Michael's, which is the name of the boy at the side of the road, view of this same event."

Early that morning Michael was out on his bike delivering the morning newspaper. As he was riding along the road, a large truck swerved and almost hit him. The wind from the passing truck caused the bike to sway and the newspapers that were loaded on the back made it impossible for Michael to keep the bike from going off the road. He careened down the side of the road into a ravine and smashed into a tree. The impact threw him off of the bike and flipped him into the air. He landed with such force that one of his legs was broken. He passed out from the pain. When he awoke, his leg was hurting so badly he could hardly move. He spent hours slowly pulling himself up the side of the ravine back to the road. He spent over an hour waving at passing cars, but he was so well hidden in the weeds that no one stopped. His leg was bleeding and he was becoming very weak. As a last desperate move he decided to throw rocks at passing cars to see if he could get their attention. Unfortunately, most cars were going so fast that no one noticed. When a car finally came by that was driving slower than the others, Michael gave it his best shot. He was relieved when the rock hit the car, but disappointed when the car kept on going.

Now ask the class "How does this new information affect what you were thinking about the kid who was lying in the weeds?"

DISCUSSION IDEAS:

"What" Questions
- Are both people in this story telling the truth as they saw it?
- At what point did you start to reconsider how you felt about Michael?

"So What" Questions
- Why can two people see the same event and feel differently about it?
- Can two people with different stories both be right?
- What is the difference between "listening" to someone and "understanding" what they are saying?
- How do our past experiences influence how we feel about an event?

- Why is it important to see things from the other person's point of view?
- What does it mean to "walk a mile in someone else's shoes"?

"Now What" Questions
- How can listening and understanding help us solve a conflict?
- Why is it beneficial to consider a problem from the others person's point of view?

TNT IDEA: With older students, using the cardboard demonstration is optional.

I DIDN'T KNOW THAT

TOPIC AREA: Self-Esteem, Team Building

CONCEPT: This activity allows you to address two different areas. The first is self esteem. Kids need to talk about their lives. Talking about themselves is an affirming behavior that reinforces the fact that each one of us has value and is worth being listened to. Being listened to is an important factor in a person's life. We have seen numerous examples of kids across the country who have felt isolated and alone because they weren't listened to and therefore felt they had little or no value. The other area that this activity addresses is team building. By getting to know each other we are able to be more productive as we work together, both in and out of class. Personal information can help break down barriers that can hinder our interpersonal relationships. You can't appreciate someone if you don't know anything about them.

METHOD: Classroom activity

TIME ESTIMATE: 15 minutes plus discussion time

MATERIALS NEEDED:
- 1 pen or pencil per participant
- 1 piece of paper per participate
- A watch
- A blackboard or large piece of tablet paper

ACTIVITY: Give each participant a piece of paper and

a writing utensil. Explain that the challenge of the activity is to talk to as many people as possible during a five minute time period. Instruct them to approach each person and ask "Tell me something about you that I don't know." Have them write down the person's first name and record their answer. They don't need to write down the entire answer, just enough so they will remember what the answer was. They must then tell the other person something about themselves. Now here comes an important part. Each time a person tells someone something about themselves, it must be something different. It must still be true but it can't be anything that they have told anyone else already during the activity. The answers may be about something they have done, something they have, something they like, something about their family, etc.

At the end of the designated time period, have each person report out how many people they were able to receive answers from. Next have them look over their list of answers and have them choose one interesting item of information that they learned. Go around the group and have each person share that one item from their list. You will have to decide if you want them to reveal who they received the item from. You don't want this to turn into a contest to see who is the most interesting person in the group. Record all of the interesting pieces of information on the board or on a large piece of tablet paper. If an item has already been listed, then the person must choose a different item to share.

DISCUSSION IDEAS:

"What" Questions
- How did the number of people you talked to compare

with the others in the class?

- How hard was it to keep thinking up new things to tell people?
- Which answer did you give that you liked the best?

"So What" Questions

- How does knowing about each other make us feel more connected?
- What happens when people feel they are not connected to other people?
- How does listening to someone make them feel?
- Do people like to talk about themselves? Why or why not?
- What is meant by the statement "Everyone has a story to tell"?

"Now What" Questions

- What is the best way to get to know someone else?
- How can learning about one another help us work together?
- How can we help a person feel connected?

I REMEMBER – WE REMEMBER

TOPIC AREA: Working Together

CONCEPT: Why do we advocate working together? What can a group of people accomplish that a single person working alone couldn't do just as well? What does the statement "Two heads are better than one" really mean? Working together is not just a phrase that makes people feel better. By combining our efforts we really can accomplish more than we can individually. There is a certain synergy that comes from combining our talents. The brainstorming of ideas is more efficient when more than one brain is involved. People bring different talents to the table and can use those talents as part of a group to better solve problems or create solutions.

METHOD: Classroom activity

TIME ESTIMATE: 20 minutes plus discussion time

MATERIALS NEEDED:
- A pen or pencil for each person
- A piece of paper for each person
- 6 teacher-created lists of words
- A watch with a second hand

ACTIVITY: You will need to prepare six lists of words before starting the activity. The first two lists should have fifteen words on them. The next two lists should have twenty words on them and the last two lists should have thirty words on them. You may write the lists on overhead transparencies or large sheets of paper. You will use the lists one at a time, so they must be on separate sheets with a way to cover up and uncover the words. You can utilize random words or you can use words that are part of lessons that you have been studying.

To begin the activity, give each person a piece of paper and a writing utensil. Explain that you are going to show them a list of words. They will have thirty seconds to study the list. They may not do any writing during the study time. After the thirty second study time, the object will be for them to write down as many words as they can remember from the list. You can adjust the times to meet the ability level of your group. Now uncover one of the lists of fifteen words for thirty seconds. Let them study the list. After covering the list back up, give them thirty to forty-five seconds to write what they remember. After the writing period, uncover the list again and have them count how many words they got correct. For every word that is correct, they get one thousand points. Share the results with the entire group. Repeat the process a second time with a new list of fifteen words.

For the next round have them get with a partner. Repeat the process twice, using the lists of twenty words. They will use one piece of paper between the two of them and only one person may write down words.
For the last round have them get in groups of four. Repeat the process using the lists of thirty words. Once again they will use one piece of paper for the entire group and only one person may write down words.

DISCUSSION IDEAS:

"What" Questions
- How many words were you able to remember when you worked alone?
- How many words were you able to remember when you were working with a partner?
- How many words were you able to remember when you worked in a group?
- What techniques did you use when you worked alone to help you remember?
- What techniques did you use when you worked with others to help you remember?

"So What" Questions
- How does this activity show that working together helps to increase what we can do?
- What made your scores go up as other people helped create the list?
- What does the phrase "Two heads are better than one" mean?
- How can people from different backgrounds help us to solve problems?

"Now What" Questions
- How can working together improve our results?
- What can we do if we want to complete a job faster or better?

IT'S KNOT EASY

TOPIC AREA: Problem Solving, Working Together

CONCEPT: Working together as a team to solve a problem is a common scenario in today's workplace. It involves not only critical thinking to decide what has to be accomplished to solve the problem, but also moving past the thinking stage to see if your solution is practical and workable. Sometimes one person has the solution and explains to the group what to do, and other times the solution is arrived at with the input of many minds. No matter how good a solution sounds, the real test is does it work. If successful, great. If not, then back to the drawing board to try it again. Learning is really an outgrowth of our past experiences. We can learn from both our failures and our successes.

METHOD: Classroom activity

TIME ESTIMATE: 15 minutes plus discussion time

MATERIALS NEEDED:
- 1 twenty foot rope per team of five. (It works better if you use a rope that is at least 3/16 inch in diameter.)
- A watch with a second hand on it

ACTIVITY: Before you start the activity, take each rope and loosely tie four knots along its length. The knots should be somewhat evenly spaced along the rope. Start the first one about four feet from one end and then tie

another knot every four feet along the length of the rope. Do not tie the knots too tightly. A single overhand knot will do nicely.

Divide your group into teams of five. Have each team stand in a single file line. Everyone should face the same direction. Lay one knotted rope down on the floor next to each team so it is parallel with how the team is standing. The two people on the ends should stand at each end of the rope and the three in the middle should each stand midway between a knot. Now instruct each person to reach down with the hand that is next to the rope and pick the rope up. (See illustration) Their challenge is to untie the knots in the rope without moving their hands along the rope or letting go of the rope. When the groups begin, start keeping time. Let each group know how long it took them to complete the challenge. Have them repeat the activity to see if they can improve their time. To save on time, allow each group to tie their own knots for the second round.

SOLUTION: The participants will have to loosen each knot one at a time and create a hole big enough in the knot so that they can untie it by passing the loosened part of the knot over the bodies of each team member one at a time.

DISCUSSION IDEAS:

"What" Questions
- How long did it take your team to complete the challenge in the first round? In the second round?
- What did you do differently in the second round?
- What was the most difficult part of the activity?

"So What" Questions
- How did your team decide what to do to solve the problem?
- Was everyone on the team involved in solving the problem? Why or why not?
- How well did your group work together?
- What happens when a group does not work well together?
- How can an individual hurt a team effort?
- What does the team need to do when their first effort is not successful?
- Is it a sign of failure when you try something and it doesn't work?
- How much easier was it to solve the problem the second time around? Why? What can that tell us about problems we encounter in everyday life?

- What can we learn from our failures? Our successes?

"Now What" Questions
- How does working together help solve problems?
- What can an individual do to contribute to the success of a team?

KING OF DEATH

TOPIC AREA: Tobacco

CONCEPT: There is always a lot of talk about how many people are killed by drunk drivers or how drugs can kill you. However, the reality is that smoking kills more Americans than any other cause of death. Smoking kills more Americans than traffic accidents, illegal drug use, fires, murder, suicide, and AIDS combined. Yet even with these overwhelming statistics cigarettes are legal, and therefore their use promoted, in the United States. We have also seen that whenever laws are written to limit their use, a cry of protest is heard from across the country. With health care concerns growing and health care costs soaring, one would think that the number one preventable cause of death would be more effectively addressed. This activity will help make children and youth more aware of the magnitude of the smoking problem. The number of deaths per year were taken from statistics provided by the Centers for Disease Control and Prevention, the National Highway Traffic Safety Administration, the National Center for Health Statistics, FBI Uniform Crime Reports and the National Safety Council.

METHOD: Classroom demonstration

TIME ESTIMATE: 3 minutes plus discussion time

MATERIALS NEEDED:
*   A metal bucket or pan

- 1,798 BBs
- 9 sandwich bags or film containers

ACTIVITY: The demonstration consists of pouring BBs into a metal container. Each BB will represent one death that happened that day due to the particular cause of death. You will need to count out the BBs and put them in containers before you begin the demonstration. You can use plastic sandwich bags or the containers that 35 mm film comes in to hold the BBs. Fill the containers with the following numbers. Put each amount into a different container and label it. Heroin/Morphine: 7, Cocaine/Crack: 9, Fire: 10, Murder: 46, Suicide: 85, AIDS: 92, Car Accidents: 114, Alcohol: 288, Smoking: 1,147. If time is an issue, for the larger numbers you can just make an estimate. The effect will still be the same.

Once you have counted out the BBs and put them into their containers, you are ready for the demonstration. Place the metal container on a table. Have the students close their eyes. Explain that you are going to pour BBs into the container. Each BB they hear land will represent one person that dies each day of the year due to various causes. Then explain that the first one they will hear is how many people will die today due to the use of heroin and morphine. Then pour the seven BBs into the container slowly enough that they can hear the individual BBs hitting the metal. After you finish pouring out each container, tell the total number of deaths that will happen that day which were caused by that method. Continue this same process for each of the other categories. Start with the lower numbers and end with tobacco. The sound of all of those BBs hitting the container is very effective in getting the point across that smoking kills more people per day than any other cause of death.

DISCUSSION IDEAS:

"What" Questions
- Did anyone try to count the BBs as they were falling? How easy was it to do that?
- Did the number for any of the causes of death surprise you?
- What were you thinking as the sound for smoking was happening?
- How many of you knew that smoking was the leading cause of death per year?

"So What" Questions
- What does this activity tell you about smoking?
- Why do people start smoking?
- Why do you think smokers keep smoking even after they are told that cigarettes can kill them?
- How do people try to influence someone to try smoking?
- How do the cigarette companies try to get people to start smoking?
- How easy is it to stop smoking once you have started?

"Now What" Questions
- What is the best way to be sure that you don't die from smoking?
- What are some ways that you can say "No" when asked to try smoking?
- How can you help a friend not smoke?

LUCKY LADY

TOPIC AREA: Goal Setting, Responsibility

CONCEPT: By not setting goals, we merely react to the events that happen to us each day. This results in us making decisions based on daily circumstances, rather than a long range plan. Many people believe that luck plays a major role in their lives rather than taking responsibility for what happens to them. Webster's Dictionary says that luck is "the seemingly chance happening of events that affect someone". When we take control of our lives and make decisions based on the goals we have set then we realize that luck doesn't control our lives, we do. The result of this realization is that we quit waiting for good luck to strike and start making our own luck. This concept reminds me a of quote that I saw on the back of a tee shirt that said "The harder I work the luckier I get". A person needs to understand that the more complex the situation is, the less likelihood there is that luck will help them be successful. The way to succeed in a complex world is by setting goals and then taking personal responsibility to reach your goals.

METHOD: Classroom activity

TIME ESTIMATE: 10 minutes plus discussion time

MATERIALS NEEDED:
- A piece of paper for each person
- A pen or pencil for each person
- A coin for each person

ACTIVITY: Give each person a coin. Instruct them that they are to flip their coins ten times. (As a suggestion I would recommend that instead of having them flip their coins, they shake the coin in their hands and then flip it over on the back of one hand. Flipping a coin in the air without dropping it is hard for some kids to do.) Before each flip, they must make a guess as to whether the coin will come up heads or tails. Have each person record their guess before they flip the coin and then keep track of whether they were correct or not after the coin flip. To record their guesses, they may simply use a "H" for heads and a "T" for tails. After everyone has completed their ten coin flips, have them report out to the entire group how many times they guessed correctly.

Now have each person get with a partner. They will repeat flipping their coins ten times. However, this time they are trying to guess what the results will be between the two coins. Have them once again number one through ten on their paper. Then have them make two columns. Label the first column "Me" and the second column "Partner". This time to be right, they will have to correctly guess what *both* coins will be. Both people do not have to make the same guess. The purpose of having a partner is only to provide a second coin. Each person must record their guess before the coins are flipped. Both partners should flip their coins at the same time. After all pairs have completed their ten coin flips, have each person report out to the entire group how many times they guessed correctly. Remind them that they had to guess *both* coins correctly to be right.

DISCUSSION IDEAS:

"What" Questions
- How easy was it to guess correctly when there was one coin?
- How easy was it to guess when there were two coins?
- What method did you use to make your guess?
- How did your scores compare with the rest of the group?

"So What" Questions
- How would you define luck?
- What part did luck play in this activity?
- What part does luck play in our lives?
- Can we depend on luck to make us succeed in reaching our goals?
- How can we make the odds better that we achieve our goals?
- Whose responsibility is it to make our own luck?
- How important is personal responsibility in reaching our goals?
- How can this responsibility be exhibited in our behavior?

"Now What" Questions
- How can we best reach our goals?
- What steps can we take to reach our goals?
- What role does personal responsibility play in reaching our goals?

TNT IDEA: Conduct one more round with three coins.

MARBLE TUNNEL

TOPIC AREA: **Problem Solving, Working Together**

CONCEPT: The old way of doing business was individual achievement. The new mantra of the workplace is teaming. Working together as a team to solve a problem is a common scenario in today's workplace. It involves not only critical thinking to decide what has to be accomplished to solve the problem, but also moving past the thinking stage to see if your solution is practical and workable. Sometimes one person has the solution and explains to the group what to do, and other times the solution is arrived at with the input of many minds. No matter how good a solution sounds, the real test is does it work. If successful, great! If not, then back to the drawing board to try it again.

METHOD: Classroom activity

TIME ESTIMATE: 10 minutes plus discussion time

MATERIALS NEEDED:
- 1 standard sized marble per team of eight
- 1 grocery bag per team of eight
- 1 piece of paper (8½ x 11) per participant
- Masking tape
- A watch with a second hand

ACTIVITY: Give each participant a piece of paper and about three inches of masking tape. Have them roll the paper into a long tube. The paper should be rolled so that the tube is 11 inches in length. The tube should be about one and a half inches in diameter. This diameter will allow a marble to pass easily through it. Use the tape to keep the tube rolled up. If there are any loose ends of the paper inside either end of the tube that would stop the marble from rolling through, tape those down also.

Divide your group into teams of eight. Mark off a starting line and a finishing line. The lines should be about twenty feet apart. Place a grocery bag for each team at the finish line. Have the teams line up single file with the first person standing at the starting line and the other team members standing shoulder to shoulder heading towards the finish line, even though

they won't extend all the way to the finish line. Explain that their challenge will be to move the marble from the starting line to the finish line and have it end up in the grocery bag. The marble must be moved by rolling it through the tubes. This will require the team members to keep moving to the end of the line as the marble rolls from tube to tube. After the marble has passed through the first person's tube, they will have to quickly reposition themselves down to the end of the line to allow the marble to keep moving towards the finish line.

No one may not touch the marble with their hands, any other part of their body or by any means other than the paper tubes. If the marble is touched or hits the ground, the team must go back to the starting line and start over again. If the time that you have allotted for the activity is running out, you may add penalty seconds instead of having them start over. This is a timed event. Read out each team's time as they finish and at the conclusion have each team report their time to the group. Repeat the activity a second time to allow for improvement.

DISCUSSION IDEAS:

"What" Questions
- How long did your team take in the first round? The second round?
- What method did you use to move the marble?
- What did you do differently in the second round? Was it successful?

"So What" Questions
- How did your team decide what to do?

- Was everyone on the team involved in solving the challenge? Why or why not?
- How did your group work well together?
- What happens when a group does not work well together?
- How can an individual hurt a team effort?
- What does the team need to do when their first effort is not successful?
- Is it a sign of failure when you try something and it doesn't work?
- How can we learn from our failures? Our successes?

"Now What" Questions
- How does working together help to solve problems?
- What can an individual do to contribute to the success of a team?

MARSHMALLOW TOWER REVISITED

TOPIC AREA: Problem Solving, Working Together

CONCEPT: In my first book, *Activities That Teach*, there is an activity called "Marshmallow Tower". This activity revisits the concepts that were addressed there with a new twist on the activity. Over the years I have used many variations of the tower activity, but this particular variation has proven to be a popular one. Students will look at the issue of problem solving while trying to create the tower. They will also have to determine ways to work together since this activity sets up an artificial situation that requires them to do so.

METHOD: Classroom activity

TIME ESTIMATE: 20 minutes plus discussion time

MATERIALS NEEDED:
- A watch
- 75 round toothpicks per team of three
- 75 miniature marshmallows per team of three
- A ruler for each team of three (you can get by with just one ruler for the entire group, but it will add to the time that the activity takes)
- Optional - A sandwich bag per team of three

ACTIVITY: Divide your group into teams of three. Give each group 75 toothpicks and 75 marshmallows. To save time, you might want to prepare these ahead of time and place them in sandwich bags. With bags you will just have to hand each team a bag containing their materials. I would also suggest that you allow the marshmallows to sit out of the bag they came in for an hour or so before you use or package them. This allows the marshmallows to harden somewhat and they are a little easier to build with.

Explain that the object for each team is to build the tallest, free standing tower that they can in the time allowed. They may only use the materials that they have been given. Warn them that the tower must stand on its own for fifteen seconds at the end of the time limit before they will be allowed to measure it. Assign numbers to each team member. During round one, person number one is the only one that is allowed to talk. Person number one may not participate in the actual building of the tower. All person number one may do is talk. Person number two and three may not talk and they may only use one hand to build with. Their other hand must be behind their back. At the end of each three minute building round, rotate who is the person that doesn't build, but can talk. Between rounds, allow thirty seconds for everyone on the team to talk about their tower. Do not count this as part of their building time. The team may hold their tower up during this discussion period, but they may not do any building.

The building time starts with sixty seconds of planning time. During the planning they may not open or touch the building materials, but everyone may talk. Once the sixty seconds are over, they may begin building. This means that they only have nine minutes of actual building time. You will stop them at the end of three minutes of their building time and at the end of six minutes so they can rotate the roles within their team. Count down the last sixty seconds of the total building time so they will know when they must take their hands off of the tower for the fifteen second waiting period before measuring. They must remove their hands immediately when you call time. Once the fifteen second waiting period is over, have them measure their tower. Have everyone look at the other teams' towers to see what approach each team used to meet the challenge.

DISCUSSION IDEAS:

"What" Questions
- How tall did your tower end up being?
- How well did you utilize your planning time?
- Did the plan change after you started building? In what way?
- Did everyone provide input to the plan?
- How did you feel when you were the one that could talk?
- Which of the two roles, talking or building, did you like the best? The least? Why?
- What happened in your group as time was running out?
- If you were to repeat this activity what would you do differently?

"So What" Questions
- Did you look at what other teams were doing to get ideas? Would that be considered cheating? (Mention that this would not be cheating. You did not tell them they couldn't look. It is a good practice to use good ideas no matter where they come from)
- How did this activity force you to work together?

- What can this activity tell us about working together?
- What problems were created by only allowing one person to talk?
- What methods did you use to communicate with other team members when you couldn't talk?
- How frustrating was it to have to rely on others to build the tower?
- What problems can occur when you work in groups?

"Now What" Questions
- How does working together help us solve problems better?
- What behaviors should you exhibit when working as a part of a team?
- How important is communication with your team members?

MEASURING UP

TOPIC AREA: Respect, Responsibility

CONCEPT: Rules, guidelines, laws: why do we have them and what good are they? What purpose do they serve? Consider a society without any laws. What would traffic look like? How would we buy and sell things? What if we had a set of rules but no one followed them? What if only some people followed them? The issue of following the rules in your family, school and community is an important one. Rules help us to function more smoothly. The rules and laws that we have are to be used by each person to help them decide what behavior is acceptable and what behavior isn't. They are a measuring stick by which we gauge our actions. It is our set of laws that gives us a standard that keeps our society from chaos. We must respect the law and make it the responsibility of each person to uphold the law.

METHOD: Classroom activity

TIME ESTIMATE: 10 minutes plus discussion time

MATERIALS NEEDED:
- A tape measure, ruler or yardstick for every two people (This can be done with just one measuring device for the entire group, it just takes longer)
- 1 small piece of paper for every two people
- 1 pen or pencil for every two people

ACTIVITY: This is a measuring activity. You will need to select a number of distances to be measured. Each team's distance to measure is must be far enough that they will have a hard time figuring out the exact length. Make each distance at least fifteen feet or more. An example would be from a certain desk to the wall or from a certain chair to another chair. It works best if you do not have more than one team measuring the same distance. Therefore, select as many distances to be measured as you have teams. Each team will be made up of two people. You do not have to have an exact measurement of each distance before starting the activity.

To begin the activity have everyone get a partner. Each team should have a writing utensil and a small piece of paper. Assign each team a different distance to be measured. In step one have each team guess how far their distance is, without allowing them to measure it or mark it off. They should make their guess to the closest half inch and record it on their piece of paper. If the partners cannot agree on the distance, then they may write down two different estimates.. After completing step one have each team report out to the entire group how far they think their distance is. For step two, allow them to measure the distance using only their bodies (feet, hands, body height, etc.). They may not use any materials from their pockets or from around the room. Once again they may make a team or individual guess. Have each group report out their estimate again.

Give each team a measuring device and have them actually measure the distance. First have them compare their estimate in step one with the actual distance and then compare their answer from step two with the actual distance. Have them determine how far off they were in each step. Report the differences from each step to the entire group.

DISCUSSION IDEAS:

"What" Questions
- How did you make your first estimate? Did you and your partner agree?
- What method did you use to make your measurement? Did you and your partner agree?
- How accurate were you in steps one and two?
- If you were to repeat this activity what would you do differently?

"So What" Questions
- How easy was it to figure out the distance without a measuring device?
- Why was it easier to measure the distance when you used a measuring device?
- A measuring device is a standard by which we measure distance. How can we compare that to laws which measure our behavior?
- Why would we need a standard by which to measure our behavior?
- What effect does the speed limit have on traffic?
- What effect do stoplights have on traffic?
- What would happen if we didn't have speed limits or stop lights?
- What would happen if people ignored the laws regarding speed and stopping?
- What would happen if everyone was able to make up their own laws to live by?
- What are some of the rules that you have in your family?
- What are some of the rules you have at your school?
- What are some of the laws that help to run your community?
- Why do we have to have police officers?

- If you were King or Queen for a day, what one law would you pass?
- If you think a rule or law is unfair, what should you do about it?

"Now What" Questions
- How do rules and laws provide a standard by which we make decisions?
- How does respect for rules and the law help our school and community?
- Whose responsibility is it to follow the rules and laws?

MIND GAMES

**TOPIC AREA: Anger Management, Media
Influence, Peer Pressure**

CONCEPT: Manipulation - the process of a person trying to influence or control someone else. Manipulation
happens all around us. Adults manipulate kids, kids
manipulate other kids and the media manipulates
everyone. Whether this manipulation is done consciously or subconsciously doesn't matter; it still happens and in many cases is very effective. Our students
need to realize that this type of activity is taking place
so they can guard against falling victim to it. Peer pressure usually takes the form of one person or a group of
people trying to manipulate the behavior of someone
else. When a person becomes angry it is usually the
result of someone else pushing their "hot button". If we
are able to recognize when someone else is trying to
manipulate us, then we can take appropriate action to
avoid placing ourselves under their influence or control.
You will need to define the word manipulation before
you begin the discussion portion of the activity.

METHOD: Classroom demonstration

TIME ESTIMATE: 5 minutes plus discussion time

MATERIALS NEEDED:
- 2 decks of cards
- 2 envelopes

ACTIVITY: Before the activity, divide one of the decks into two groups. In one group have all of the diamonds and spades and in the other group have all of the hearts and clubs. Then from a second deck, take the King of Diamonds and the Queen of Clubs and place each one in a separate envelope and seal the two envelopes. Be sure that you know which card is in which envelope. Now you are ready to begin.

Choose one person, at random, from your group to come up and volunteer. Hold up one of the envelopes (the one with the King of Diamonds in it) and declare to the group that you are going to help your volunteer read your mind and they will know what card is in this envelope. Tell them that you know which card is in the envelope, but the volunteer doesn't. However by sending mental messages from your brain to theirs, they will be able to select exactly the card that you are thinking of and that you have already placed in the envelope. Play up the fact that the volunteer has no previous knowledge of which card is in the envelope. Then place the envelope down where everyone can keep their eye on it. Now hand the volunteer the group of cards that is made up of only the diamonds and spades. Have the volunteer show the cards to the group. Tell the audience that they must remain perfectly silent during this process or they will ruin the "mind melding" that needs to take place between you and the volunteer. Ask the volunteer, "Are you ready?" "Then let's begin!"

Ask the volunteer to mentally select the color red or black. If they select black, then ask them to remove all of the black cards from their hand and place them on the floor or a table. If they select red, than ask them to keep all of the red cards in their hand and remove the black ones and place them on the floor or a table.

Now ask them to mentally select either the numbered cards (2-10) or the face cards (Jack - Ace). Be sure to explain that the Ace is a face card. If they select the numbered cards, then ask them to remove all of the numbered cards from their hand and place them on the floor or a table and keep the rest of the cards. If they select the face cards, ask them to keep all of the face cards and discard the other cards by placing them on the floor or table.

Now ask them to mentally select the lower two face cards (Jack and Queen) or the upper two face cards (King and Ace). If the select the lower two face cards, ask them to remove them from their hand and place them on the floor or table and keep the rest of the cards. If they select the upper two cards, ask them to keep those two cards and discard the other two cards by placing them on the floor or table.

Now ask them to select the King or the Ace. If they select the Ace, ask them to remove that card and place it on the floor or table and keep the other one. If they select the King, ask them to keep that card and discard the other one by placing it on the floor or table.

You are now ready to have the envelope opened and reveal the enclosed card. Magically, it will be the same one (the King of Diamonds) that the volunteer is holding in their hand.

Repeat the same sequence with the second group of cards, the second envelope and a new volunteer. However, this time the suits will change as will the final sequence since you have a different card in the envelope. The key to this activity is to have them always keep the cards that will lead to the card that is in the envelope and discard the cards that won't. Just remember to have them always discard the color or cards that won't match what is in the envelope. When the volunteer makes a choice, you will have to determine whether you want them to keep the cards they chose or discard the cards that they chose. Keep the process moving quickly or what you are doing might become too apparent. Practice the process a few times at home before trying it with your groups.

Explain to the group the secret of what you were doing. Show how even though the volunteer was the one making the choices, you manipulated them into doing what you wanted them to do.

DISCUSSION IDEAS:

"What" Questions
- What were you thinking as the process was going on?
- Did you figure out the secret before I revealed it?
- Does it seem easy now that you know how to do it? Could you do this trick?

"So What" Questions
- Can other people manipulate you into doing things? Why or why not?
- What kinds of tricks do people use to try and get others to do what they want them to?
- Do people have certain "hot buttons" that make them angry?
- How can others use these hot buttons to make someone angry?
- How is peer pressure a form of manipulation?
- How does the media manipulate people?

- What are some tricks that advertisers use to manipulate people?

"Now What" Questions
- What can you do to avoid allowing others to manipulate you?
- What role does peer pressure play in manipulation?
- What can you do to stop people from successfully pushing your "hot buttons?"
- How can you stop the media from manipulating you?

MONA LISA

TOPIC AREA: **Diversity, Team Building**

CONCEPT: Each person is unique. If we were all the same, with similar interests, backgrounds, skills and characteristics, our society would be missing much of its creativity. This diversity allows for multiple points of view, with the end result being various perspectives to problems or solutions. Telling students that they are unique seems to gloss over what actually makes them unique. By discussing various topics on how we are unique, we can get kids thinking about diversity and how valuable that is for society.

Here is a story that I use to help introduce this activity. I was sitting at the McDonald's restaurant on Cheyenne Blvd in Las Vegas eating breakfast when a very tall man came through the door. The man turned out to be Mark Eaton who used to play basketball for the Utah Jazz. Mark Eaton is 7 feet 4 inches tall. When he sat down at a table his legs stuck out into the aisle and his feet went into the booth across the aisle. He is one tall person! If you were forming a basketball team would you want Mark Eaton on your team? Well of course! Now think about horse racing. If you needed a jockey for your horse would you choose Mark Eaton? Probably not because his feet would drag on the ground and slow your horse down. How about if you needed an astronaut? Well Mark probably wouldn't fit in the space capsule, so he would get very cold. I would probably choose someone else. So the bottom line is that Mark Eaton is a good size for a basketball player but too large to be a jockey or an astronaut. That is the same way it is in our society. This is not to say that Mark Eaton couldn't be a jockey or an astronaut but certain people can meet some of our needs better than others, and without all types of people we lose some of the characteristics that make us the strong country that we are.

METHOD: Classroom activity

TIME ESTIMATE: 30 minutes plus discussion time

MATERIALS NEEDED:
- A pen or pencil for each person (Crayons or colored pencils may also be used.)
- 2 large (8½ x 11) pieces of paper for each person
- 1 small (2 x 3 inches) piece of paper for each person
- Masking tape

ACTIVITY: Write everyone's name on a small piece of paper. Put only one name on each piece. Give everyone a large piece of paper and something to draw with. Randomly distribute the papers with names on them. Have everyone check to be sure that they didn't get their own name. If they did, collect their paper (along with four or five others) and redistribute them. If everyone in your group doesn't know everyone else's name, then have each person say their first name. This will give everybody a chance to match up the name on their paper with the appropriate person. Emphasize that no one is to let anyone else know whose name they have received.

Explain that each person is to draw a picture, from the neck up, of the person whose name they received.

Give them a time limit that you will allow them to draw (about four or five minutes). Once they have all completed their drawings, tape them on the wall. Write a number on the bottom of each picture. Each person must prepare an answer sheet with as many numbers as there are pictures. Have everyone look at the pictures and write down on their answer sheet next to that picture's number who they think the picture is of. When everyone has made their choices, reveal the correct answers. You can do this by first asking who the person was that drew the picture and then having them reveal the name of the person they drew. For each correct guess, participants receive one thousand points.

DISCUSSION IDEAS:

"What" Questions
- How many did you get right?
- Were you able to guess yourself correctly?
- What facial feature was the hardest to draw?
- Which features helped you the most to determine who was pictured?

"So What" Questions
- List ways in which people are the same.
- List ways in which people are different.
- How can people be similar but not the same?
- Can all differences between people be seen when you look at someone? Why not?
- Why is it important to have different types of people in your town? In your school?
- Why is it important to have different types of people as your friends?
- If we were all the same, what kind of a world would we have?

- How does being different help us sometimes and hurt us sometimes?
- Do people always respect how unique each of us are? Explain.

"Now What" Questions
- How should we treat people who might be different than we are?
- How can we keep differences that you can see from affecting how you think about a person?

TNT IDEA: Emphasize that this is not a contest to see who can draw the best. Everyone should just do their best.

MOST OR MOMENT?

TOPIC AREA: **Alcohol and Drugs, Decision Making, Goal Setting, Sexuality**

CONCEPT: We all have goals in our lives. Some people write these goals down and others just have a vague notion of them floating around in their minds. Many of our goals are short term things that we want to accomplish. But some goals are of the long term nature. Our students do not realize that reaching a long term goal is really determined by the day-to-day decisions they make. The decisions that they make have consequences and these consequences will help determine if their long term goals are met or not. The question they will need to answer on a daily basis is whether what they want today is more important than what they want in the future. They need to consider how the choices they make today will affect their goals of tomorrow. Some examples of poor choices would be alcohol and drug use, sexual activity which could result in sexually transmitted diseases or pregnancy, watching television at the expense of doing your homework, etc.

METHOD: Classroom demonstration

TIME ESTIMATE: 10 minutes plus discussion time

MATERIALS NEEDED:
- 1 piece of paper per participant
- 1 pen or pencil per participant
- 2 pennies, a nickel, a dime, a quarter and a dollar bill

(You will give away the quarter)
* A dollar bill wrapped up in a box like a present (You might give away another quarter or the dollar bill)

ACTIVITY: Before the activity, wrap up a dollar bill in a box so that it looks like a present. To begin the activity, give each person a piece of paper and a writing utensil. Have everyone write down five goals they would like to accomplish in the next five to ten years. Explain that these should be goals they would be willing to share with a partner. Now have them share their goals with a partner. Then ask them to write down one goal that would make them the happiest they could ever imagine being. Explain that this goal will not be shared with anyone.

Once this has been accomplished, have a student come forward to help you with a demonstration. Hold out your hands with a penny in one and a nickel in the other. Ask the student "Which coin would you rather have, the penny or the nickel?" If they choose the penny, thank them and have them sit down and start over with another student. If they ask for the nickel, then give it to them. Now put away the penny and bring out a dime. Ask "Which would you rather have, the nickel that is in your hand or this dime?" If they want the dime, give it to them and take back the nickel. Now bring out a quarter and ask "Which would you rather have, the dime that is in your hand or this quarter?" If they want the quarter, give it to them and take back the dime. Thank them for their help and have them return to their seat.

Ask another person to help you. Tell this person that you will be offering them money also. However you also have this box. Bring out the box that is wrapped up like a present. Explain that they can either take the money that you offer them or they can hold out and get what is in the box at the very end. If they agree to accept any amount of money as you offer it to them, then they will not be offered the box at the end. Ask them, "Do you want a penny or do you want to hold out for the box?" Then ask, "Do you want a nickel or do you want to hold out for the box?" Ask, "Do you want a dime or do you wish to hold out for the box?" "Do you want a quarter or do you wish to hold out for the box?" If at anytime they accept the money, then thank them and have them return to their seat. You will then reveal what was in the box. Ask them "Now that you see what you gave up, do you wish you would have held out for the box?"

If they have refused all offers to take the money than state, "Because of the decisions you have made, you are now eligible for the what is in the box. Do you wish to accept what is in the box?" Then give them the box and have them open it. As your final question ask, "Are you glad that you waited for what was in the box?" Then thank them for their participation. Emphasize that if the person had taken any of the coins that were offered to them, they would have been happy for the moment. However, they would have been disappointed later because they gave up something better for what made them happy at the moment.

Now have everyone write on the bottom of their paper this statement "The chief cause of unhappiness and failure is sacrificing what is wanted most for what is wanted at the moment." Have them keep their papers and post them somewhere at home where they can be reminded not to sacrifice their long term happiness by the daily decisions that they make. As a reminder of this lesson, you can make a poster that says "Moment or Most?" to post where your students will see it often.

DISCUSSION IDEAS:

"What" Questions
- How hard was it to create your list of five goals?
- What was one interesting goal that you heard from your partner?
- Did you have a hard time thinking of one goal that would make you the happiest to achieve?
- Would you have made the same choices as the volunteers did?

"So What" Questions
- In the second round, why did they hold out for the box instead of taking one of the other coins?
- How can this be compared to decisions we make?
- Who is responsible for the decisions that we make?
- How do the decisions we make everyday affect our long term goals?
- What are some behaviors that would prevent us from reaching our goals?
- How would using alcohol or other drugs affect us?
- How would becoming involved in sexual activity affect us?
- How would neglecting our education affect us?
- Do the decisions that we make impact others around us? How?
- Describe a situation where someone made a decision that shows they care more about their immediate happiness than their future?
- Describe a situation where someone made a decision that shows they care more about their future than their immediate happiness?

- What role does peer pressure play in making decisions that are not helpful to us in the long term?
- What is meant by the statement "The chief cause of unhappiness and failure is sacrificing what is wanted most for what is wanted at the moment."?
- Define the term "delayed gratification".

"Now What" Questions
- How can having long term goals help us make good daily decisions?
- Describe how the decisions you make today can change your future?

The concept for this activity was given to me by Holly Wamsley from Taylorsville, Utah. Thanks Holly.

MY LIFE

TOPIC AREA: **Self-Esteem, Team Building, Violence**

CONCEPT: Talking about ourselves is not something we do easily. Kids seem to think that if you talk about yourself you are bragging or trying to sound important. However, a teacher-structured activity which allows people to talk about their lives in a non-threatening manner allows sharing without the problems sometimes associated with such talk. Telling others about what we do, what we think and what we believe is a good way to affirm that each person is important and that their thoughts and lives are worth sharing. This activity also allows people to get to know each other better. This type of dialogue can help break down barriers between individuals and groups. Barriers can lead to a number of problems such as stereotyping and violence. Understanding how others think and realizing that we all have a lot in common can help us relate to each other.

This activity can also be used as part of a communication lesson where you want your students to practice good listening skills.

METHOD: Classroom activity

TIME ESTIMATE: About 30 seconds per participant plus discussion time

MATERIALS NEEDED:
- A watch with a second hand

ACTIVITY: Have your group count off, one-two-one-two, etc. Have them form two circles, one inside of the other. The inside circle should be facing out and the outside circle should be facing in. (See illustration) Each person must have a partner across from them. If you have an uneven number of participants, then you will need to play since everyone needs to have a partner. Explain that you will read out a question or statement to the group. The inside person will complete the statement first and then the person on the outside circle will complete the same statement. Each person will have about ten seconds to talk. Wait two to three seconds after announcing the question before having them begin to talk. This will give them a chance to consider their answers. They must keep talking for the entire time. You can determine what the right amount of time would be for your group. If they have answered the basic question and there is still time left, then have them elaborate or expand on their answer.

The teacher or leader will keep track of the time and call out when each person's time has expired. To refresh their memory, repeat the statement before the second person's turn to respond. After both partners have had their turn, it is time to rotate. Have the inside circle stay put and the outside circle move one person to the right. Then repeat the process with a new statement. You can use the statements that I have listed or create your own. Continue until you have completed one revolution of the circle.

- My favorite comic book super hero is _____ because.....

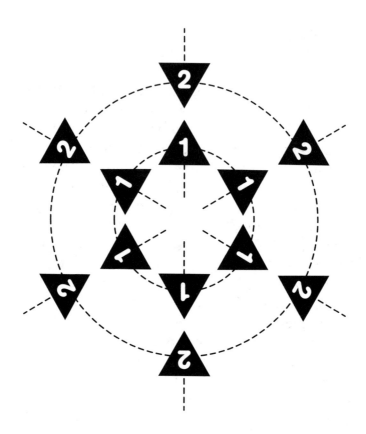

- My favorite sport to play or watch is
  _____ because.....
- If I could go anywhere on vacation, it would be
  to.....
- The worst thing about morning is
  _____ because.....
- If I could be any animal, I would choose
  _____ because.....
- The subject in school that I enjoy the most is
  _____ because.....
- The subject in school that I enjoy the least is
  _____ because.....
- Five years from now I would like to be doing.....

- If I could give up one bad habit, it would be...
- If I could change one thing at this school, it would be.....
- If I could change one thing about the world, it would be.....
- If I were the President of the United States, I would.....
- If I were the Principal of my school, I would.....
- If I only had six months to live, I would.....
- The person I would most like to have dinner with is_____ because.....
- If I could go back in time, it would be to the year_____ because.....
- If I could live anywhere in the world, it would be _____ because.....
- If I could have any job, I would choose _____ because.....
- The best definition of success is.....
- The most important thing in my life is.....
- My parents always.....
- If I had a million dollars, I would.....
- I have always wanted to.....
- One of the things that makes me angry is.....
- I hate it when.....
- Some of the things I like about weekends are.....

DISCUSSION IDEAS:

"What" Questions
- How hard was it to think of your answers?
- Was it hard to concentrate on your partner's answers when you were going to be next?
- Which question did you have the most trouble with?
- Which question did you enjoy answering?

"So What" Questions

- Is sharing your own thoughts with others a worthwhile thing to do? Why or why not?
- Is listening to others about what they think a valuable way to spend your time? Why or why not?
- How does being listened to make a person feel?
- Do people like to share their thoughts and feelings? Why or why not?
- What kinds of people are easiest to talk to?
- Did you find that others had answers similar to yours?
- How does getting to know each other help us avoid problems?
- How does getting to know each other help break down barriers between different groups?
- How can getting to know people from groups other than our own help reduce violence?

"Now What" Questions

- How can we help someone feel good about themselves?
- What is the best way to get to know someone?

MY TURN?

TOPIC AREA: **Communication, Goal Setting, Problem Solving, Working Together**

CONCEPT: When you get right down to it, goal setting is really a problem solving activity. You want to get something that you don't have. This could be something material such as a car or it may be more behavioral such as losing weight. The "what" will vary from person to person and for that matter even from year to year as we age and our lives keep changing. However, your goals may change but the process for reaching them remain the same. You need to have a plan. You can't expect to move towards your goal unless you create a list of steps that will allow you to move in the appropriate direction. This aspect of goal setting involves problem solving. It is the creation of a workable plan that stops many of our young people from reaching their goals. Instead of coming to fruition their goals simply remain dreams or wishes. By creating a plan and then communicating the plan to others, your students will have a much more realistic chance of achieving their goals.

METHOD: Classroom activity

TIME ESTIMATE: 10 minutes plus discussion time

MATERIALS NEEDED:
- Each participant must be sitting in a chair or at a desk
- A watch with a second hand

ACTIVITY: Divide into groups of ten to fifteen. Form a circle with each member of the group sitting in a chair. Have everyone close their eyes and keep them closed while you explain the activity. Tell them that their challenge is to count to the number (15 or 20). They will do this as a group. Each person will stand up (rising at least six inches off their chair) and call out a number. The numbers must be called out in consecutive order. The group may not pre-arrange who is going to say which numbers. There is no talking other than the calling out of numbers allowed. The choice of who is going to call out the next number must be completely at random. If you see anyone pointing or talking, then call them on it and have the group start again. Caution them that they may not go around the circle in order. Each time any two people begin to stand at the same time or say a number at the same time, the entire group must begin all over again. They can't repeat the same order of people when starting over. Every person in the group must say at least one number.

If you have only one group, then you be the judge. If you have two or more groups, you will need to rotate the position of judge among the participants. Be very strict about the rules They will probably have to start over again a number of times before they finally meet the challenge After about ten tries, tell them that they have only two more chances to complete the challenge. If by some miracle they complete this challenge on the first try, tell them that you want them to do it again without using the same order, but try to get it done in a shorter period of time.

Now explain that in the second round you are going to let them discuss strategies before they try it again.

They still can't go around the circle go in order. Give them about ninety seconds to discuss strategy. After they have decided upon a strategy, time how long it takes them to complete the challenge If they want to try two different strategies to see which one is faster, let them.

Now in round three they are going to use the simplest strategy. They will just go around the circle and have each person count off. They still must rise slightly from their chair when they say their number. Time them a couple of times to see if they can break their own record.

DISCUSSION IDEAS:

"What" Questions
- How many tries did it take us to get it right in the first round?
- Did the same people always try to go early in the challenge?
- What was your strategy as to when you would stand up during the first round of the challenge?
- What was our final record time?
- What could we do different to make our time even faster?

"So What" Questions
- What made round one so difficult?
- What made round two easier?
- Why was round three the fastest round?
- What can we learn about communication from this activity?
- What can we learn about the importance of having a plan from this activity?

- Which type of plan usually works better a complicated one or an easy to understand one? Why?
- How does working together help when trying to solve a problem?
- Why do you need a plan to reach your goals?

"Now What" Questions
- How can working together help us solve a problem?
- How does having a plan help you reach your goals?
- How can you use communication to help reach your goals?

PARENTS WANTED

TOPIC AREA: Sexuality

CONCEPT: Reducing teen pregnancy is not an easy challenge. While some studies show that births to teens are on the decline, the numbers are still way too high. Of course most people who work with youth realize that reducing the number of births is not the only issue An additional objective is to reduce teen sexual activity since this may result in sexually transmitted diseases, emotional trauma and other problems. While teen sexual activity is a difficult topic to address, this activity uses a non-threatening approach that will allow the opportunity to discuss the issue at various age levels. Students can discuss the qualities that they think make a good parent and understand that they may not yet possess these qualities. It is not that they will never have these qualities, but that sometimes age determines whether you have the quality or not. Being able to provide financial support is one important quality of a good parent, yet most teenagers do not have the ability to get or keep a good paying job.

METHOD: Classroom activity and demonstration

TIME ESTIMATE: 15 minutes plus discussion time

MATERIALS NEEDED:
- 1 piece of paper for every two people
- 1 writing utensil for every two people
- 10 toothpicks

ACTIVITY: Have everyone get with a partner. Each pair will need a piece of paper and a writing utensil. Read the following scenario.

Last night a five-day old baby girl was found abandoned on the steps of the police station in a small town. After a thorough search for the little girl's parents produced no results, the police chief chose to put the baby up for adoption. The police chief would like to find the "perfect parents" for this little girl and has decided to take out an advertisement in the local newspaper. However, he is not sure what the qualities of "perfect parents" are since he has never had children of his own. Your challenge is to write a newspaper advertisement that would describe a set of "perfect parents". You must list at least five qualities and after each quality you must comment on how that quality would benefit the little girl as she grows up.

After reading this scenario, give the students about three to five minutes to write their advertisement. Ask them to prioritize their list. Then have each advertisement read out loud. Have each pair indicate which of the qualities they have named would be the most important one. Write each pairs' most important quality on the board. If there is too much repetition, ask for an alternative choice.

Finish with this demonstration. Pick up the ten toothpicks one at a time. Each time you pick up a toothpick, read one of the qualities that you have written on the board. Explain that each toothpick will represent the quality that you name as you pick it up. When you have all ten toothpicks in your hand, hold them in a bundle and try to break them all at once. You will not be able to break them if they are held together and form one tight bundle. If you would like, you may have one of the students be the one that tries to break the toothpicks. Just be sure that they are held in a tight bundle as the student is trying to break them. You may use more than ten toothpicks if you prefer. Now take one toothpick at a time out of the bundle. Once again relate the removal of the toothpick with one of the qualities that you have written on the board. After removing one toothpick, try again to break the bundle. Continue removing toothpicks and naming qualities that are being lost. Eventually you will be able to break the toothpicks when their numbers have been sufficiently reduced. Emphasize that as you reduce the number of toothpicks you are simulating a reduction in the number of qualities that the parents possess.

DISCUSSION IDEAS:

"What" Questions
- How hard was it to think of the qualities to write down?
- Could you have listed more than the required five qualities?
- How closely did your qualities match what other pairs had decided upon?
- How difficult was it to prioritize your list of qualities?

"So What" Questions
- What are the qualities of a good parent?
- How do you get these qualities if you don't have them now?
- Choose three qualities and indicate at what age most people acquire these qualities?

- What happens to the babies as they grow up if some of these qualities are missing in their parents?
- How many qualities would the parent have to be missing before that would hamper the development of the child?
- Why wasn't I able to break the toothpicks when I had so many of them bundled together?
- How can we compare that demonstration to the number of good qualities a parent has?

"Now What" Questions
- How can we best ensure that children will have a happy childhood?
- At what age do you think a person has the best chance to have the qualities needed to be a good parent?

PROBLEM ATTACK

TOPIC AREA: **Conflict Resolution, Respect**

CONCEPT: When people get mad or angry at someone, they have a tendency to attack the person with everything they've got. This usually includes calling the person names such as "stupid", "idiot" and worse along with generalizing about what that person has done wrong in the past using such phrases as "you always" or "you never". This approach to solving a conflict never gets them anywhere except into a bigger and more heated dispute.

Many programs teach the concept of using "I messages" or "I statements" when dealing with conflict resolution because using these types of statements direct the argument or conflict away from attacking the person and moves the discussion to attacking the problem. An "I message" or "I statement" usually consists of the following phrase. "I feel _____ when _____ because _____". An example would be "I feel angry when you cut in front of me in the cafeteria line because it makes me wait longer for my lunch." As opposed to a "you statement" which says "You are such an idiot, you always cut in line front of me." The technique of attacking the problem and not the person will help to solve the conflict rather than escalating it and shows respect for the people involved. This activity will help you to reinforce that concept. The discussion of this activity will be more productive if you discuss the above mentioned information before you conduct the activity.

METHOD: Classroom activity

TIME ESTIMATE: 15 minutes plus discussion time

MATERIALS NEEDED:
- 3 empty soda pop cans for each team of five
- 3 pieces of 8½ x 11 paper for each team of five
- Masking Tape

ACTIVITY: Divide your group into teams of five. Create a starting line on the floor with masking tape. Give each team three empty soda pop cans and have them make a pyramid out of them (two cans on the bottom and one on the top) about five feet (can be adjusted depending upon your age group) from the starting line. Give each team three pieces of paper and have them make three balls by crumpling each piece of paper. Now have each team line up single file behind the starting line opposite from their pyramid of cans. The object will be for them to try to knock the top can off of the pile without knocking over either of the bottom two cans. For each top can they knock off without knocking over a bottom can, the team receives 100 points. Each player will make three throws and then the line rotates. They may throw overhand or underhand. Explain that the top can represents the problem when trying to solve a conflict. The bottom two cans represent the people that are involved in the conflict. In solving a conflict it is necessary to talk about the problem or the issue, but it is not OK to attack the people involved.

After each person completes their three throws they are to go out and retrieve the paper balls, give them to the next person in line and then take their place at the back of the line. When the entire team has had a chance

to throw, the round is over. Give them one practice round, before the official scoring round, to get the feel of challenge. Report out the team scores to the group. If time permits, you can conduct an additional round to see if their scores improve.

DISCUSSION IDEAS:

"What" Questions
- How many points did your team score?
- What throwing method did you use?
- Did you make any changes in how you threw the paper balls? Did it help?

"So What" Questions
- What happens when you are trying to solve a problem and people begin name-calling?

- How does name-calling get in the way of solving a conflict?
- How can talking about a problem help to solve the problem?
- How do "I statements" or "I messages" help to solve a conflict?
- How does using "I statements" or "I messages" show respect for others?

"Now What" Questions

- How can we avoid attacking the person when trying to solve a conflict?
- What should we concentrate on when trying to solve a conflict?

REACH FOR THE STARS

TOPIC AREAS: Achievement, Goal Setting, Responsibility

CONCEPT: We want students to achieve all they can with the skills and abilities they have. This activity can be used to discuss the fact that no matter how well someone is doing right now, they could probably do better with a little more effort. Maybe the problem isn't that they need to try harder, but they need to try "smarter". If they are studying in front of the television set for one hour and they want to improve their grades, maybe spending two hours studying in front of the television set wouldn't be as beneficial as spending only one hour studying without the television. Sometimes it's not the amount of effort we put into a project as much as it is how smart we are in that effort. Rather than just trying harder to reach your goals, think about what you can do differently to reach your goals.

Responsibility also plays a role in achieving what we want. It is up to the individual to put out the effort and to seek solutions to any problems which come up. Placing blame outside of ourselves for failing to attain our goal is usually called an excuse rather than a reason. This is not to say that we will always get what we want, but it is a call to give 100% effort and to use all of the resources that are available to us rather than giving a half-hearted effort and calling it quits.

METHOD: Classroom activity

TIME ESTIMATE: 10 minutes plus discussion time

MATERIALS NEEDED:
* Masking tape
* A wall

ACTIVITY: Give each person their own three small pieces of masking tape about one inch in length. Have them place the pieces of tape on their arm or clothing where they will be able to pull them off when needed. Have everyone get a partner. Determine who will be partner A and who will be partner B. Now ask each pair to get next to a wall with partner A standing right next to the wall and facing the wall. Partner B will stand about two to three feet behind partner A. Once they are all in position ask partner A to remove one of the pieces of tape from their arm. Their challenge is to stick that piece of tape on the wall as high as they possibly can. While doing this they must keep their feet flat on the floor. Explain that this is not a competition against each other since there are obvious height differences. After all of the A's have placed their first piece of tape, have the B's take their place at the wall and place their piece of tape.

Now go on to round two. Explain that you are going to repeat the process. Have partner A make another attempt using their second piece of tape and see if they can beat their first effort. During this round partner B should cheer them on and encourage them to try to beat their first effort. Now switch places and repeat the process. Remember that they must keep both feet flat on the floor. Have everyone step back and look at the

results from the first two rounds. Most people will have surpassed their first attempt.

For round three repeat the process again except that they no longer have to keep their feet flat on the ground when placing their third piece of tape. They may jump, hop, stand on their tip toes, etc. Do not allow their partner to physically help them. Their partner should cheer them on, but not provide a boost. Everyone will be able to reach higher than they did when they had to stand with their feet flat on the floor and just reach.

DISCUSSION IDEAS:

"What" Questions
- How high did you reach the first time?
- How high did you reach the second time?
- How high did you reach when you didn't have to keep your feet flat on the ground?
- In round three what method did you use to get even higher?

"So What" Questions
- Why were you able to reach higher the second time?
- Would you agree that you tried harder the second time? Why or why not?
- How did having the masking tape there from round one help you reach higher in round two?
- How did having your partner cheer you on help your effort?
- Why were you able to reach even higher when you didn't have to keep your feet flat on the ground?
- What can this activity tell us about "trying harder?"
- How can having specific goals help us to achieve more?
- Explain this statement: "If we always do what we've always done, we'll always get what we've always got."

"Now What" Questions
- What can we do instead of just "trying harder" to reach our goals?
- How can thinking or acting differently help us to achieve our goals?
- Who is most responsible for us reaching our goals?

REMOTE CONTROL

TOPIC AREA: Decision Making, Peer Pressure, Responsibility

CONCEPT: Each of us is a special and unique individual, but other people certainly influence what we do and who we become. When we are young, our parents play a major role in deciding what we will wear, what we will eat and how we will spend our free time. As we get older, others such as our friends, older brothers or sisters and other significant adults begin to usurp the influence that our parents had. However, we must realize that even though friends and others are important to us, a person can lose their own "self" as they try to mold themselves to fit into certain groups. This process may manifest itself in such harmless areas as how you dress or wear your hair, but it could also have a significant impact in areas such as reaching your goals, school achievement, sexual activity, alcohol and other drug use, etc. if one isn't careful.

The more personal responsibility you assume for your decisions and lifestyle, the less negative effect others will have on your life. It is not harmful to seek input from others or look to someone else as a mentor or role model, but you must be aware what effect others have on your life so you don't fall into the trap of becoming someone you don't wish to be. By taking personal responsibility, you will not rely on others to make your decisions for you or do things that you aren't really comfortable with just to be one of the crowd. This activity will give kids a chance to look at what would happen to their lives if they let others make decisions for them.

METHOD: Classroom activity

TIME ESTIMATE: 12 minutes plus discussion time

MATERIALS NEEDED:
- 1 piece of paper per person
- 1 pen or pencil per person
- 1 dice per team of six

ACTIVITY: Give everyone a piece of paper and a writing utensil and tell them to number one through six on the piece of paper. Have them label this list as "My Answers". Read through the following questions and have each person write their answers on their own piece of paper.
- What is your favorite food?
- What is your favorite television show?
- What is your favorite sport?
- What is your favorite color?
- If you could choose any animal for a pet, what would it be?
- If you could choose any job to have when you are older, what would it be?

After answering the questions, have them form groups of six. Each group will need a dice. Have them make a new list of the numbers one through six on their own piece of paper and label this list as "Group Answers". Now assign one number, starting with one and going through six, to each person in the group. If due to the number of participants a team does not have six players, then assign two numbers to some people.

The person who has been assigned number one will roll the dice first. Whatever number it lands on, the person who has been assigned that number will read out their answer for question number one. That now becomes the group answer for the first question. Everyone will write down that person's answer on their own piece of paper next to number one on the new list labeled "Group Answers". Now the dice passes to person number two. They will roll the dice. Once again, whatever number it lands on the person that has been assigned that number will read out their answer for number two and everyone will write that answer down on their piece of paper next to number two. You continue this process until you have gone through all six numbers. When completed, have each person compare their set of "My Answers" with the "Group Answers".

DISCUSSION IDEAS:

"What" Questions
- Which question was the easiest for you to answer?
- Which question did you have the hardest time answering?
- How did your first personal list of answers compare with the group list?
- Do you like the answers on the group list?
- If you answered these same questions a year from now would the answers be the same? Five years? Ten Years? Why or why not?

"So What" Questions
- In what ways do others have control over your life?
- In what ways do others influence your life?
- What is the difference between control and influence?

- How much influence do others have over the things that you do?
- Who has the most influence over the things that you do?
- Will the same people still influence you as you get older?
- How does peer pressure affect the decisions we make?
- How can changing how we act just to fit in with the crowd get us into trouble?
- Who is ultimately responsible for the decisions we make and the consequences? Why?

"Now What" Questions
- How can we be sure that the influence of others is positive rather than negative?
- How can our decisions reflect what we believe and not what others believe?
- What is wrong with changing how we behave just to fit in with the crowd?

SCHOOL OF HARD KNOCKS

TOPIC AREA: **Respect, Responsibility**

CONCEPT: "Respect your elders". This is a phrase that has been around for a long time. But why should young people do so? The most common answer would probably be because they have lived longer and have gained wisdom that younger people can benefit from. How can we transmit that wisdom from one generation to the next generation? The easiest way would be to just ask them what they experienced.

When kids hear "respect your elders", their response is often "why?" To be honest, respect usually has to be earned. One way the older generation can earn that respect is to show that they have met the challenges of life and become wiser because of those experiences. Then after their wisdom has been shared, it is the responsibility of the younger generation to act upon that shared information.

METHOD: Classroom activity

TIME ESTIMATE: This must be done as a homework assignment. The next day you will spend about 20 minutes in small groups plus processing time.

MATERIALS NEEDED:
- A piece of paper per person
- A writing utensil per person

ACTIVITY: Your students are going to become newspaper reporters. Their assignment is to interview someone who is at least twenty years older than they are. They must write the answers down and share them the next day with others in the class. You want them to ask questions that allow them to learn something about life from the person they are interviewing. You may make up the list of questions or you may use some from the following list. You should have them ask about three to five questions.

• Describe a time when you had a lot of fun.
• Describe a challenge that you overcame in your life.
• How would you define success?
• What advice would you give young people today?
• Who was an influential person in your life? Why?
• What classes did you take in school that have helped you in life? How have they helped?
• What is the secret to getting along with other people?
• What should I look for in a person to marry?
• How does a person earn respect?
• How would you define a good parent?

When the students return to class, have them get into groups of four or five. Have them go through the list of questions and have each person share the answers that they received with their group. Before proceeding to the next question, have each group share the most interesting answer heard within their group with the rest of the class. If time is at a premium, just have a couple of groups share after each question. If you choose this option, have each group choose an answer and then you call on various groups to share with the entire class. If you only take volunteers, some groups will not make an effort to determine which answer they would like to share.

DISCUSSION IDEAS:

"What" Questions
- How hard was it to find a person to interview?
- How easy was it for your interviewed person to answer the questions?
- Which question was your favorite?
- Did you ask any follow-up questions to find out more about a certain answer?
- Did you ask any additional questions?

"So What" Questions
- Can other people make us listen to their advice?
- What is the difference between listening and hearing?
- How do we show respect to our elders?
- How do people gain our respect?
- How do people lose our respect?
- How hard is it to gain back respect once it is lost?
- What was the most interesting thing that you learned?

"Now What" Questions
- What behaviors show our respect for others?
- How can people older than you help you succeed in life?
- How can you use this information in your life?

SHERLOCK HOLMES

TOPIC AREAS: Respect, Stereotyping

CONCEPT: How do we form our opinions of others? Many times we let first impressions influence what we think. These first impressions may be based on a person's clothes, the way they talk, where they live, their religion or the color of their skin. However, how accurate are first impressions? Have we based our impression on things we have believed about how a group of people look and act? Do we put people into categories such as "preppies", "jocks", "nerds", "stoners" etc. based only on what we see?

One way to respect others is to care enough about them to take the time to get to know them before making judgments about who they are and what they think. When you lump everyone into stereotypical groups based on what you see, you reduce them to a one-dimensional definition instead of the complex person they really are. We should not draw conclusions about a person based only on what we see or hear about them. We must also realize that others may be stereotyping us by how we look or act. Are we making the impression we want?

METHOD: Classroom activity

TIME ESTIMATE: 20 minutes plus discussion time

MATERIALS NEEDED:
- A piece of paper for each team of two
- A pen or pencil for each team of two
- A variety of objects you have collected
- A description of three different people
- 3 grocery bags

ACTIVITY: Prior to starting the activity you will need to do some planning. Look around your house and gather up a number of items that could belong to a fictional person that you are going to create. Let me give you an example of the kinds of items I would collect. The items would be things that I would find in a person's bedroom. They could include: a fishing bobber, a hunting knife, a leather keychain with the name Tom stamped into it, a compass, an address book with a religious symbol on the front and a pair of men's glasses.

After collecting the items, I would create a fictional person to go along with these items. The items could reflect the following about this person: the person is a female, she is a teenager, she likes to fish, hunt and hike, she has a lot of friends, she is religious, she has a boyfriend named Tom and her father left his glasses in her room last night when he was using the computer. Since the items don't always reflect something specifically about the person, you can create anything that fits the items you have collected. Notice that I tricked the group by using the pair of men's glasses. These did not belong to the person, but were found in her bedroom. After you gather some items, you will need to make a list of the characteristics that go along with your fictional characters. You will want them to be vague enough that there will be many interpretations of what the person is like based on the items you show. As you will see, it won't be until the third round when the class can ask questions that their guesses will be close to the fictional person's characteristics.

Repeat this process of collecting items and creating a person two more times. You should end up with items and descriptions for three characters. Put the items for each person into separate bags so no one can see them until you are ready.

Have everyone get with a partner and give each team one piece of paper and a writing utensil. Explain that you are going to show the group a number of items that you found in a fictional person's bedroom. Their job is to take on the role of detectives and try to figure out as many things about the person as they can based on the items you are going to show them. Tell them to be as specific in their characteristics as possible. You would like for them to decide if the person is a male or female, their age, what their likes or dislikes are, what they do with their free time, any physical characteristics that they can determine, etc.

Begin by bringing one item at a time out of one of the bags. You can name the item so they will know what it is. Let them take a look at the item, but do not answer any questions about it. After bringing it out of the bag, place the item on the table or the floor where everyone can see it. Once you have brought everything out of the bag, give each team about two minutes to write down as many characteristics as they can determine about the person as possible. When the two minutes are over, ask for ten to twelve samples of the characteristics they have written down. After hearing the characteristics from various groups, have each group tell how many characteristics they listed on their paper. Now you read your list of characteristics and have them give themselves one point for each characteristic they wrote down that matches a characteristic you made up. The team with the most points is the winner of that round. Repeat the activity a second time with new items and a new fictional description.

Repeat the activity a third time with new items and a new fictional description. However, after showing them the items but before having them make their list of characteristics, allow the entire group to ask you ten questions about the person that can be answered "Yes" or "No". Anything they find out during the question and answer time can be used to make up their list of characteristics so be sure they take notes.

DISCUSSION IDEAS:

"What" Questions
- How much trouble did you have thinking of characteristics?
- Was your team's list longer or shorter than the lists of others?
- How precise were you when you listed your characteristics?
- How well did you match the correct characteristics on the first two rounds?
- How hard was it in round three to think of questions about the person to ask?
- How much easier was it to list characteristics after you were able to ask questions?

"So What" Questions

- Why was it easier to list characteristics after first asking questions?
- How much do you know about a person when you first meet them?
- What do you judge a person on when you first meet them?
- What kinds of mistakes can we make when we judge a person by just what we see?
- What is wrong with generalizing about a person by how they look or who they hang out with?
- Is hearing about a person from someone else a good way to get to know them? Why or why not?
- How does getting to know someone show that you care about them?

"Now What" Questions

- What is the best way to get to know someone?
- What is wrong with drawing conclusions about a person using just a few bits of information?

SHOE SIZE

TOPIC AREA: Conflict Resolution, Respect

CONCEPT: Many times conflict originates because we do not understand what the other person is trying to communicate to us or we do not take the time to put ourselves in their place. To solve a conflict we must take the time to understand the viewpoint of the other person. Part of this understanding is to respect the other person's feelings and the background that they bring to the problem. A person who is growing up in a home where having enough money is always an issue may see things differently than someone who is growing up in a home where there is an adequate amount of money. This can also be true for someone growing up in circumstances such as living in a single-parent family, a blended family, in a family with an alcoholic parent, as someone with a disability, a perfectionist, an overachiever, a sports enthusiast, etc. The point is that our background and environment tend to color what we think and how we respond to circumstances. What may make one person angry, may not even affect someone else. Once we learn to respect the fact that others may come from a different point of view than ours, based on their background or environment, we can use that understanding in helping to solve a conflict.

METHOD: Classroom activity

TIME ESTIMATE: 15 minutes plus discussion time

MATERIALS NEEDED:
- 1 piece of paper per person (the paper must be large enough to trace their shoe)
- 1 pen or pencil per person
- 1 small piece of paper per person

ACTIVITY: Give everyone a piece of paper and a writing utensil. Have them trace the outline of their right shoe on one side of the paper. Now have them turn the paper over. Designate the direction that the shoe is pointing as the top of the paper. In the middle of the paper put down whether they are male or female. In the upper left hand corner have them put their shoe size. In the upper right hand corner have them put their hair color. In the lower left hand corner have them put their favorite sport. In the lower right hand corner have them put their favorite color. When completed, collect the papers and place them in a circle on the floor with the shoe outline facing up. Now have everyone stand next to a piece of paper. Give them a small piece of paper for writing down their answers and keeping score.

Explain to them that they will walk around the outside of the circle of papers until you call for them to stop. Each person must stop in front of one of the papers. Have them place their right foot on the outline of the shoe. If their foot is exactly the same size as the one they are comparing it with, then they will receive ten points. After checking to see if their shoe fit, you are ready for the bonus question. Everyone gets to participate in the bonus questions whether their shoe sized matched or not. The bonus question involves the answers that have been written on the back of each paper. In the first round, they are to guess whether the person is male or female. First they must write down their answer on the small piece of paper. Then everyone turns the paper with the shoe tracing on it over and checks to see if they were right. If they get the answer right, then they receive an additional ten points. Round two begins by everyone walking around the circle again until you tell them to stop. Once again they try to fit their shoe on top of this new outline and receive ten points if it matches.

Now for the bonus question, you ask them the question that is answered on the upper left hand corner of the back of the shoe tracing which in this round is, "What is the shoe size of the person?" They will once again answer first and then check by turning over the piece of paper and reading the answer in the upper left hand corner. If correct, they receive another ten points. Continue to do this for five rounds, progressing through the answers on the back of the paper. At the end have everyone report out their scores to the group.

DISCUSSION IDEAS:

"What" Questions
- How many times did your shoe exactly on the one on the paper?
- How many times did you get the bonus question right?
- How did you score in relation to others in the group?

"So What" Questions
- What can you tell about a person from just looking at their shoe size?
- What does the saying "Walk a mile in someone else's shoes" mean?
- What problems might a person be experiencing that you can't see by just looking at them?

- How do some people try to hide their problems?
- What problems might you encounter if you were poor, rich, in a wheelchair, tall, super smart, not good in math, etc.?
- How does a person's background or environment affect how they act or think?
- How can coming from different backgrounds create conflict?
- What role does respect play in solving a conflict?

"Now What" Questions
- How can you learn more about a person?
- How does trying to understand a person's point of view show respect?
- How can understanding a person's point of view help when trying to solve a conflict?

SHORT CIRCUITED MEMORY

TOPIC AREA: Drugs, Marijuana

CONCEPT: Drug impairment is real. Young people need to realize that there are consequences to using drugs. Different kinds of drugs produce different effects in the body. Since curiosity is one of the primary reasons kids will try drugs, this activity will give you a chance to have them experience a drug consequence.

One of the areas of the brain that marijuana affects is that of memory. Specifically short term memory. The impairment of this ability decreases a person's level of performance in school, in athletics, on the job and everywhere else that requires one to think. Just as with all drugs, the level of impairment will vary with each individual due to body characteristics, genetic make-up, frequency of use and the purity of the drug itself.

METHOD: Classroom activity

TIME ESTIMATE: 5 minutes plus discussion time

MATERIALS NEEDED: None

ACTIVITY: This activity works a lot like the old game of "Simon Says". Have everyone stand up and face the leader. I have found that it works best for you to be the leader. You can vary the pace of the activity based on the age and the ability of the group. In round number one, you call out a list of body parts that you want them to touch. You do not have to say "Simon Says" nor do you touch the body part you are calling out, just call out the list. They must touch the body part that you call and continue to touch it until you call for the next body part. They may use their right or left hand to touch the body part. Once you have called the next body part, they stop touching the first one and touch the next one. A sample list of body parts would look like this: head, knee, elbow, shoulder, foot, ear, thumb, belly button. Go through this list and see how they do. Repeat a second time at a much faster rate. I suggest that you have your list written down to reduce problems for yourself in rounds two and three.

Now explain that for round two there will be one change. Instead of them touching the body part that you call out, they will wait and do that one after you have called out the next body part. Basically this means that they will always be one body part behind you. They must remember what body part you called while at the same time listening for the next body part. Here is an example using the list from round one. You call out head and they don't do anything. Next you would call out knee and they would touch their head, then you would call out elbow and they would have to touch their knee, etc. When you get to the last body part and they still have one more to touch, just call out "Next". Repeat this round so they can have a chance to really concentrate.

In the third round you would have them stay two body parts behind you. Repeat this round so they can have a chance to really concentrate. For younger grades, keep the same list for all three rounds while creating a new list for each round for the upper grades.

DISCUSSION IDEAS:

"What" Questions
- How hard was it to keep up in the first round? In the second? In the third?
- What method did you use to try and remember where to touch next in rounds two and three?
- Did you watch others to help you remember what to do next?
- On a scale of 1 - 5, with 1 being low frustration and 5 being high frustration, where would you score your feelings in each round?

"So What" Questions
- What part does memory play in this activity?
- How did your memory have to work harder in each successive round?
- What role does memory play in our everyday life?
- What kinds of problems would result in your school work if your memory was impaired?
- What kinds of problems would occur in activities outside of the classroom?
- How well would you function at the workplace if your memory was giving you problems?
- How well would a person who used marijuana be able to compete against those who are not impaired?
- What problems would you have if you worked with a person who smoked marijuana?

"Now What" Questions
- What should we do to avoid having our memory impaired?
- How does the use of marijuana impact the workplace?
- What problems would you have reaching your goals if you used marijuana?

STICKS LIKE GLUE

TOPIC AREA: Marijuana

CONCEPT: Marijuana is a fat soluble drug as opposed to a water soluble drug. Water soluble drugs can pass through your body fairly quickly. The elimination of water soluble drugs is accomplished mainly through urinating or sweating. However a fat soluble drug does not pass through the body very quickly. The THC (delta 9 tetrahydrocannabinol) found in marijuana is rapidly absorbed by the fatty areas of the body such as the brain, heart, lungs, liver and reproductive organs. THC can be detected in the fatty tissues of the body for up to thirty days after use. Since marijuana is not water soluble you can't speed up its elimination by drinking liquids, exercising or getting your body overheated to produce sweat. The passage of time is the only process that produces the elimination of THC from your body. For the discussion part of this activity to be effective, you will have to give the above mentioned or similar information to your group before you conduct the activity.

METHOD: Classroom activity

TIME ESTIMATE: 10 minutes plus discussion time

MATERIALS NEEDED:
- 10 medium-sized balloons per team of four
- Masking tape
- A watch with a second hand

ACTIVITY: Divide your group into teams of four. Explain that the challenge will be to see how many balloons each team can attach to the back of one its team members. Therefore before you even begin, each team must choose a person to be the one who will have the balloons attached to their back. (If the teams are thinking ahead, they will choose the largest person on their team since that person's back will offer the most space for attaching balloons.) Now give each team about two feet of masking tape and 10 balloons. Tell them that they will have 3 - 4 minutes (adjust the time as you watch their progress) to blow up their balloons, tie the ends and attach as many balloons as they can to the back of the chosen team member.

Each balloon must touch and be attached to the person's back. The balloons may also be taped to each other to help hold them in place. They may use only the amount of tape that they have been given, so warn them to use it wisely. To make sure that they have in fact attached the balloons with care, announce that at the end of the time all of the people with balloons on their backs will have to spin around three times. If a team finishes early, they must wait for time to expire so everyone will do the spinning at the same time. The only balloons that will count are the ones that stay on after they have finished spinning. Each team receives 100 points for every balloon that remains stuck on the back. Have each team report out their score to the group.

DISCUSSION IDEAS:

"What" Questions
- How many balloons did your team successfully stick on?

- How many balloons fell off during the spinning?
- If you were to repeat the activity, what would you do differently?

"So What" Questions
- How does this activity relate to the fact that marijuana is fat soluble?
- Why isn't marijuana flushed from the body easily?
- How does being fat soluble make a drug more harmful than if it was water soluble?
- Is there anything you can do to speed up the elimination process of a fat soluble drug? Explain
- How safe is marijuana if you only use it on the weekends? Why?
- How important are the organs of the body that are affected by the THC in marijuana?

"Now What" Questions
- What should you do to avoid the problems associated with marijuana?
- If you know someone who is using marijuana, what could you do to help them stop?

STORYTELLER

TOPIC AREAS: Conflict Resolution, Cooperation, Working Together

CONCEPT: Individual effort is appreciated, but working with others is critical in today's world. We work in teams, groups and committees all of our lives. Very few of us will work or live in a situation where we have the final say on everything. How well we are able to take the ideas of others and blend them with our own ideas will determine the success we have when working with other people. One skill that helps when being asked to work with others is creativity. Many times the solution to opposing opinions or ideas is a creative combination of those opinions. Compromise consists of taking at a number of different solutions to an issue or problem and blending them together.

In the area of conflict resolution, you may use this activity to point out that people don't always control the situations they find themselves in. Just as the story comes to them already heading in a certain direction, life too comes at them with certain circumstances already in place. They have to deal with the story and with life as it comes. The expression "When life hands you a lemon, make lemonade" can be used to point out that although you can't always control the circumstances in your life, you can control how you react to those circumstances. The issue of compromise in conflict resolution may also be addressed.

METHOD: Classroom activity

TIME ESTIMATE: 15 minutes plus discussion time

MATERIALS NEEDED:
- 20 small pieces of paper (about 2 inches by 3 inches) per team of five people with a couple of extra pieces of paper for mistakes
- A pen or pencil for each person

ACTIVITY: Divide into groups of five. Give each group two small pieces of paper and a writing utensil to each person. Ask each person to write one word on each of the pieces of paper that they were given. The words they choose must be nouns (a person, place or thing). Examples of this would be Abraham Lincoln, Michael Jordan, Hawaii, Alaska, ping pong table, canoe, etc. They are to write a different word on each piece of paper. Ask them to write clearly so that others will be able to read what they have written. Tell them not to show the word they wrote to anyone else. When completed, each group will have ten pieces of paper with ten different words. (Don't worry if by coincidence two people wrote the same word. When they have finished writing, place the papers randomly face down on a table or the floor in the middle of the group.

Explain that this is going to be a storytelling activity. To begin, have one person select one of the pieces of paper. After they have selected, have the person on their left select a piece of paper. The first person that chose a piece of paper will start telling a make believe story out loud. As they tell their story, they must at some point use the word they have drawn in the story. Even after they have used their word they must continue to tell the story until you call out that it is time to change. When you have indicated that it is time to change, the person on their left immediately picks up the story where they left off and continues it. Remind them that as they continue the story it must make sense. As with the first person, they must at some point use the word that they drew. As each person begins their turn, have the next person draw a word so they will be ready to go as soon as the story gets to them. As each person finishes their turn, they must put the word back in the middle face up to ensure they have in fact used it. Continue in this fashion until all of the words are drawn. Remind the last person that they must draw the story to a conclusion.

Repeat the activity starting over with a new set of words.

DISCUSSION IDEAS:

"What" Questions
- How hard was it to think up words to write on the piece of paper?
- How hard was it to use the word you drew in the story?
- Did the story make sense?
- How did you feel when your turn was next?
- If right before your turn the story started to go a direction you hadn't planned on, what did you do when it was your turn?

"So What" Questions
- How hard was it to pick up where someone else stopped in the story?
- Was the activity easier the second time around? Why or why not?

- Would it have been easier if you could have done the whole story by yourself?
- What part does cooperation play in this activity?
- Is it always easy to cooperate? Explain.
- Why is cooperation important?
- What are some careers that require a great deal of cooperation among its workers?
- How can creativity help us solve problems?
- Does creativity help us cooperate with one another?
- How does compromise help us to work together?
- What role does compromise play in resolving a conflict?
- Does someone have to be the winner and someone the loser when we compromise? Why?

"Now What" Questions
- How does a person act when they are not being cooperative? When they are being cooperative?
- When there is more than one opinion about how to solve a conflict, how can we use cooperation, creativity and compromise to come to an agreement?

STRESS CIRCLE

TOPIC AREA: Stress Management

CONCEPT: Everyone has stress. Problems, deadlines, expectations of others, everyday demands, etc. all create stress in our lives. However, if it wasn't for stress we wouldn't get anything done. To some degree, stress motivates us to accomplish a variety of tasks. Stress, in and of itself, is not a bad thing. Stress creates problems for people when the expectations and demands of the day are greater than our ability to deal with them. This activity will give the participants a chance to experience different levels of stress.

METHOD: Classroom activity

TIME ESTIMATE: 15 minutes plus discussion time

MATERIALS NEEDED:
- An object for each group ten people (the object will need to be small enough it can be passed around a circle from person to person such as a tennis ball or a small balloon)
- A list of categories

ACTIVITY: Divide into groups of about ten. Have each group stand in a circle or sit in a circle either in chairs or on the floor. Give each group a small object. Explain that you will be giving out a category such as vegetables or baseball teams and you will tell them how many items from that category they must list. You will be the one that decides how many items from the category they have to list. As soon as the category and number of items has been given, the person who has the object will start to pass it around the circle to the right. They must then begin listing a certain number of answers from the category that you gave them. They must give the correct number of answers before the object goes around the circle and returns to them. Only the person who starts the object may talk. If your group is made up of less than ten people and you feel the person answering needs more time, have the object go around the circle twice. If you have more than one group, you will have to appoint a judge for each group since the action will go too fast for you to hear each group. Rotate the judges in and out of the groups each round.

For the first couple of rounds, make the categories easy and the number of answers required short. For example, "Name three sports that are played with a ball", "Name four different kinds of cars", "Name four toppings that you can put on a pizza". Then increase the difficulty and the number of items that must be named. You want the activity to get progressively harder to simulate an increase in stress levels. By the end, the lists should be very difficult to complete, if not impossible. Choose your categories based upon the ability level and age of your group. Adjust the number of answers required in each round according to how many people are in the circle. If time allows, have each person be the one that has to give the answers more than once so everyone has an opportunity to have an easier and more difficult list. If you would like to create even more stress in the second round, have the person giving the answers stand in the middle of the circle while answering.

Sample categories:
- Use categories that relate to subjects that you are studying
- Sports played with a ball
- Toppings put on a pizza
- Different kinds of cars
- Different kinds of balls used in sports
- Comic book heroes
- Television shows
- Fruits
- Vegetables
- Animals with four legs
- Song titles
- Book titles
- Movie titles
- Presidents
- States
- Rivers
- Sports figures
- Music personalities
- Words that start with the letter "s"
- Foods you eat with your hands

DISCUSSION IDEAS:

"What" Questions
- How often did your group succeed?
- How easy was it to think up the correct responses?
- What category did you think was easy? Hard?
- What new category would you suggest?

"So What" Questions
- What made this activity stressful?
- Who was the person under the most stress?

- How can this activity be compared to stress in our lives?
- What are some things that create stress in our lives?
- What are the body's physical signs of stress?
- What behaviors do we exhibit when we are under too much stress?
- Does everyone react to stress the same way?
- Are the same things stressful to everyone? Why or why not?

"Now What" Questions
- What are some of the ways we can make sure we don't get too stressed out?
- What are some of the negative behaviors people use to reduce stress?
- What are some of the positive techniques we use to get through a stressful situation?
- How can we help others when they become stressed out?

TEST DAY

TOPIC AREA: Decision Making, Peer Pressure, Responsibility

CONCEPT: Cheating is widespread in our schools today. Survey after survey has shown that from elementary school to the college campus, a large number of students don't think that there is anything wrong with cheating. At the core of this problem is probably the issue of personal responsibility. If circumstances arise where cheating is called for, was it really my fault or did the circumstances themselves drive me to do it? What kinds of outside forces were making me do it? Kids have the opinion that it really isn't their fault when they cheat if they can find someone else to blame their actions on. We need to point out that each of us is responsible for our own decisions, our own actions and the consequences that follow those actions.

METHOD: Classroom activity

TIME ESTIMATE: 20 minutes plus discussion time

MATERIALS NEEDED:
- A copy of the story for each person
- (Optional) A magic marker and a large piece of paper for each group of three or four

ACTIVITY: Divide into groups of three or four. Give a copy of the story "Test Day" to each person. Read the story aloud while everyone follows along silently. Then have each group rank the characters in the story from most responsible for Helen getting in trouble to least responsible. If there is disagreement within the group as to the ranking, explain that a vote must be taken and the majority will rule. Each group should be ready to verbally defend their choices. After the groups have finished, have each group read their ranking and give their reasoning for their choices. If time is an issue, have them only give their first three choices. It is beneficial to have each group write their rankings on the board or large tablet paper so the different groups can visually compare the lists.

Test Day

Eric was not a good student because he didn't try very hard. As a matter of fact he was down right lazy. One night while watching TV he remembered there was a big test tomorrow and he hadn't studied. Eric didn't think school was very important. His parents always told him that school was only important if you wanted to be a doctor or a lawyer. They didn't care about his schoolwork. Eric decided that he would just cheat. He thought of a number of plans, but none of them were very practical. Then he remembered that when the teacher had him stay after school to make up a test, she had taken the answer key out of the file cabinet behind her desk.

The next day Eric asked some of his friends to help him steal the answer key. He asked Mike, Carlos, Janet and Shauna to help and they all agreed as long as he would share the answers with them. During lunch the boys were going to stage a shouting match in the cafeteria to distract their teacher's attention while the girls would slip back into the classroom and get the answer key out of the file cabinet and hand it out the window to

Eric. It sounded like a great plan, except that the teacher locked the classroom door as she went to lunch. The kids were discussing what to do next when Helen came and sat at their table. Helen was extremely bright and was well liked by all of her teachers.

Eric had another idea. He told Janet and Shauna to have Helen get the keys from the teacher by telling Helen that they wanted to study with her for the test during lunch and the classroom would be nice and quiet. Helen wasn't very popular with the other kids. Janet and Shauna on the other hand were very popular. Therefore when they asked her to help them study back in the classroom she agreed at once. The boys were still going to stage the shouting match and Eric would go to the window while one of the girls handed him the answer key. The girls went with Helen to ask for the keys to the classroom. The teacher was pleased they were going to give up their lunch break to study. She handed the keys over to Helen without any questions since the teacher trusted Helen. As the girls entered the classroom Eric was waiting by the window to signal Mike and Carlos to start arguing.

Helen saw Janet heading straight for the teacher's file cabinet and knew that she had been tricked. Helen started to voice her disapproval when Janet and Shauna said things like "you are so cool for doing this", and "a real friend would help us out". Helen reluctantly gave in, and handed Janet the keys to the cabinet. Just as Janet passed Shauna the answer key, the teacher walked in and caught them. The three girls were sent to the principal's office, their parents were called and they were suspended for three days and got a zero on the test.

List the order of who is most at fault to who is least at fault for Helen getting into trouble.
Eric, Mike and Carlos, Janet and Shauna, Helen, Eric's Parents and the Teacher. (Mike and Carlos count as one person. Janet and Shauna count as one person.)

DISCUSSION IDEAS:

"What" Questions
* How easy was it to get your group to agree on the ranking?
* What method did you use to get agreement in the group?
* What criteria did you use to arrive at your ranking?
* What were the main facts from the story that influenced your ranking?
* What role did Eric play in the story?
* What role did Mike and Carlos play in the story?
* What role did Janet and Shauna play in the story?
* What role did Eric's parents play in the story?
* What role did the teacher play in the story?

"So What" Questions
* How much influence do others have on our actions?
* What impact does what our friends think have on our behavior?
* Do circumstances control what we do? Why or why not?
* Do circumstances influence what we do? Why or why not?
* Who controls your thinking?
* Who is responsible for the decisions that we make?
* Who is responsible for the consequences of our behavior?

- Should the girls have told about what the boys had done? Why or why not?
- Should the boys have turned themselves in? Why or why not?

"Now What" Questions
- How can we be sure that others aren't influencing our decisions and behavior in a negative manner?
- How can we be responsible for our own behavior?

This activity was adapted from a story by LaMar Macklin of Panguitch, Utah. Thanks LaMar!

THAT'S NOT FAIR

TOPIC AREA: Achievement, Judging Others

CONCEPT: "That's not fair!" How often have you heard that phrase? Well life isn't always fair. Resources, such as money, time, power, ability, etc., are not spread evenly throughout our society. Some people have more and some people have less. Does that mean that those that have been given more should look down on those who have ended up with less? Should those that have less give up and not even try to realize their dreams? Uneven distribution of resources does not mean that some people are better than others nor does it give some people the right to take advantage of others to get more. The story is often told about someone who turns to crime or selling drugs because they don't have the ways or means to support themselves using traditional avenues. Tragedy or unforeseen circumstances can also strike and take away what you have. What makes some people fight back after a tragedy while others give up?

METHOD: Classroom activity

TIME ESTIMATE: 20 minutes plus discussion time

MATERIALS NEEDED:
- 32 straws per team of three (These are easily acquired at your local fast food outlet. Let the manager know what you will be using them for and they will usually be donated.)
- Masking tape

- 1 piece of paper per team of three with messages already written
- 1 ruler per team
- 1 paper bag per team

ACTIVITY: You will need to do some preparation before hand. First prepare the materials for each team. Have some extra materials. Each team will not receive the same amount of materials. Vary the number of straws per team from a low of sixteen to a high of forty-eight. Give them approximately ½ inch of masking tape per straw. For example, a team that received sixteen straws would get eight inches of masking tape. Put all of the materials for each team in a paper bag so the variations in supplies won't be noticeable immediately. Also prepare a message for each team. Write on different pieces of paper the following messages:

- Your team is doing a good job. Keep it up!
- Your tower has experienced an earthquake and was completely destroyed. Go up to the teacher, get a new set of building materials and start over again.
- During construction, strong winds blew away one half of the straws that you have left. Take one half of your remaining straws and turn them into the teacher.
- You have been given a business award by the city. You can go take two straws from any team you wish (the straws must not already be part of their tower).
- You have been given a grant by the city. You may go up to the teacher and receive four extra straws.
- The worker's union has declared a silence strike against your building company. Your team members may not talk for the rest of the building time.
- A shipping error has been made. You can go up to the teacher and receive an extra six inches of masking tape.

- All of your workers have been injured in a freak accident. From now on they can only use their left hands.

You will prepare enough of these messages so that each team will receive one. Depending on how large your group is, some teams may receive the same message. After you write these messages, fold the papers and staple them shut.

Now you are ready to begin. Divide your group into teams of two or three. Explain that their goal is to build the tallest freestanding tower that they can using only the materials you have given them. Randomly pass out sets of materials to each group. They will have about 10 minutes of actual building time to complete their tower. Adjust this time according to the abilities of your group. Do not count the time you spend distributing the messages as part of the building time. At the end of the building time the tower must stand by itself for fifteen seconds before they can measure it. When teams notice that the materials have not been evenly distributed, just explain that you are aware of that fact and they should do the best they can with what they have.

Half way through the building process, stop the group. Ask them to send one member from each team up to the front and give them one of the messages that you have prepared. Have them wait until everyone has returned to their groups so that all of the messages will be opened at the same time. Then continue the building process with whatever changes the messages have called for. At the end of the building time, wait fifteen seconds to be sure that the towers have been sturdily built and then measure to see which tower was the tallest.

DISCUSSION IDEAS:

"What" Questions
- How tall was your tower?
- How was your building plan developed?
- If you were to design your tower over again, what changes would you make?
- If you would have had more materials, would your tower have been taller?

"So What" Questions
- How did you feel when you noticed some teams had more or less materials than your team?
- How would you have felt if your team was given a grade on who had the tallest tower?
- Would grading the towers on how tall they were be fair? Why or why not?
- What can this activity tell us about people and the resources that they have to work with?
- What are some circumstances that give some people more and some people less resources to work with?
- Describe some situations where some people have an advantage over others due to money or power.
- Do we always have control over our circumstances? Why or why not?
- Do the amount of resources that we have determine how much we will be able to achieve in life? Why or why not?
- How do resources influence our thinking?
- Is it important to consider individual circumstances before judging other people?

"Now What" Questions
- How should we react when faced with less resources than others? With more resources?
- What are some things that we can do to help us understand someone else's circumstances?

THEY SMOKE WHAT?

TOPIC AREA: Responsibility, Tobacco

CONCEPT: The ingredients and chemicals found inside a cigarette are harmful to your body. These ingredients and chemicals go far beyond the most commonly known items which are tar and nicotine. It is true that nicotine is the chemical that causes you to become addicted, but it is not the only harmful chemical found in tobacco. The same ingredients that are found in cigarettes are also found in a number of household items. For example you will find steric acid in mascara, aftershave and skin lotion. You will find butane in deodorant and hair spray. You will find formaldehyde in shampoo and nail polish. You will find acetone in nail polish remover. You will find ammonia in window cleaner and spray starch products.

Tobacco smoke has additional chemicals which include cadmium that is used in artist's oil paints and produces yellow stains on teeth. You will find hydrogen cyanide which is used as a gas chamber poison and affects breathing. There is vinyl chloride out of which plastic garbage bags are made and can make your fingers turn white and hurt when cold. You will find toluene which is an embalmer's glue that can inflame and crack your skin. There is benzene which is found in rubber cement and can cause drowsiness, dizziness, headaches and nausea. Also found is the chemical arsenic which is used in rat poison.

Are these the chemicals you want in your body? Would you purposely seek out these chemicals and swallow them? If you smoke cigarettes then these and many other chemicals are finding their way into your system. The best way to stop that from happening is to not smoke! This is a choice that must be made by each person. Advertisements, movies or celebrities should not be making this decision for you.

METHOD: Classroom activity

TIME ESTIMATE: 10 minutes plus discussion time

MATERIALS NEEDED: None

ACTIVITY: Explain to the class that you are going to list some of the main ingredients that are found in a number of foods or household items. Their challenge will be to decide which item is being described.

For the first two items you will read the list of ingredients aloud and accept guesses from the students.
- 1st item: Potatoes, vegetable oil, soybean oil and salt. (Potato Chips)
- 2nd item: Flour, water, yeast, soybean oil, tomatoes, onions, cheese and pepperoni. (Pepperoni Pizza)

For the next five items you will give them a choice. Have them indicate their choice by going to one side of the room or the other.
- 3rd item: Are these ingredients found in an oatmeal cookie or an Oreo cookie? (Oreo cookie)
  Sugar, flour, riboflavin, vegetable shortening, cocoa, corn syrup, vanilla and chocolate.
- 4th item: Are these ingredients found in Fruit Loops or Frosted Flakes cereal? (Fruit Loops)

Corn, wheat, oat flour, sugar, vegetable oil, salt, corn syrup, red dye #40, blue dye #1, yellow dye #6
- 5th item: Are these ingredients found in a Hot Dog or Cat Food? (Cat Food)
  Beef, eggs, potassium chloride, salt, caramel color, water, sodium nitrite
- 6th item: Are these ingredients found in Peanut Butter or a Baby Ruth Candy Bar? (Baby Ruth Candy Bar)
  Sugar, roasted peanuts, corn syrup, soy bean oil, milk, cocoa, caramel coloring
- 7th item: Are these ingredients found in Soap or Fingernail Polish? (Fingernail Polish)
  acetate, formaldehyde, fiberglass, alcohol, artificial colors

For the 8th item, have them guess what the product it is. Accept answers by taking guesses from the group.
- 8th item: What product are these items found in? (Tobacco)
  Acetone, ammonia, arsenic, butane, carbon monoxide, formaldehyde, hydrogen cyanide, methane, propane

DISCUSSION IDEAS:

"What" Questions
- Were most of your guesses correct or incorrect?
- Which item was the easiest for you to guess?
- Which item was the hardest for you to guess?
- Which item had the ingredients that surprised you the most?

"So What" Questions

- Do the chemicals that are found in tobacco sound like they would be harmful to your body?
- Are these chemicals ones that you want in your body?
- Would you purposely seek out these chemicals and swallow them?
- How do other people try to influence someone to try smoking?
- How do the cigarette companies try to get people to smoke?
- Why do you think smokers keep smoking even after they are told that the chemicals in cigarettes can hurt them?
- What is meant by the term "addicted"?
- What is the chemical in cigarettes that causes you to become addicted?
- How easy is it to stop smoking once you have started?

"Now What" Questions

- What is the best way to avoid becoming addicted to cigarettes?
- To avoid the chemicals found in cigarettes, what is a good answer to give someone who asks if you want to smoke?
- Who is responsible for a person's decision to smoke or not to smoke?
- How can you help someone else to never try smoking? To stop smoking?

THREE TOGETHER

**TOPIC AREA: Problem Solving, Working
                    Together**

CONCEPT: Being able to work together as part of a team to solve problems is one of the characteristics that today's companies are looking for in their employees. People who lack the ability to look at problems from a number of angles or are locked into simply following someone else's instructions are not going to easily survive or advance in today's information age. We need to allow our students opportunities to experience solving problems that have no easy or right solution.

METHOD: Classroom activity

TIME ESTIMATE: 15 minutes plus discussion

MATERIALS NEEDED:
- 1 penny per team of three
- 1 - 12 inch string per person
- 1 pencil per team of three
- 1 - 8½ x 11 inch piece of paper per team of three
- A watch with a second hand

ACTIVITY: This activity must be played at a table or on the floor. Divide your group into teams of three. (If you don't have the correct number of participants, have one or two teams with only two players. Designate the right hand of one person as a player and their left hand as another player.) Give each team a penny, three twelve

EASIER  HARDER

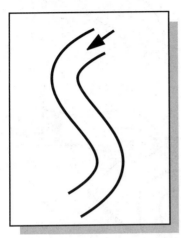
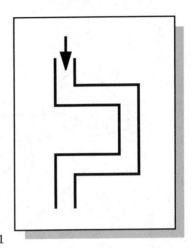

Fig. 1

inch pieces of string, a pencil and a piece of paper with the course drawn on it. You may use a copy machine to make the course ahead of time or you may draw a sample on the board and have each team copy the sample onto their piece of paper. The course should look like one of the examples in figure 1. Use the easy course for younger children. For older kids use the harder course or you may do the activity twice by starting with the easy line and then using the harder line.

Explain the challenge. Each team will try to move their penny along the course. The penny must stay between the lines of the course. The penny may only be touched by the pencil's eraser. No one may ever touch the pencil. Each person may only touch one of the three strings. (See figure 2) The paper may not be moved nor may the surface be tilted in any direction once the third phase of the challenge has begun. The first phase of the challenge is for planning. It lasts sixty seconds. During

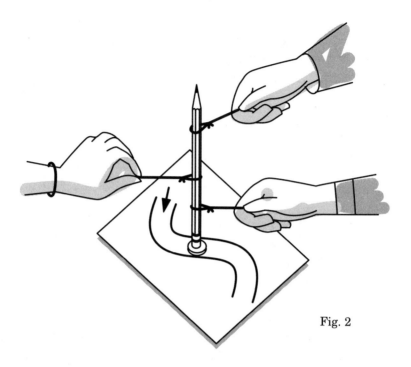

Fig. 2

this time the materials may not be touched. The second
phase is for practice. They may have two minutes to
experiment with the materials. They must follow the
rules listed above, even during this experimentation
round. During the experimentation round they may use
the strings to devise a method to move the penny. They
may practice moving the penny to see how well their ideas
work. Have everyone begin the third round together. This
is a timed round. The object is to see how fast they can
move their penny from the starting point on the paper to
the ending point while staying between the lines. As each
team finishes, read out their time. If you can see that
some teams will never be able to finish, call time.

Now give them about ninety seconds to experiment.
During this time they may improve on their design or
practice their skills. Then conduct another timed round.

For younger children: Tie the three strings onto the pencil before you explain the challenge. It will be enough of a challenge for them to get the penny moved using the three strings without the additional challenge of trying to figure out what to do with the three strings in the first place.

DISCUSSION IDEAS:

"What" Questions
- What was your first reaction to the challenge?
- How well did your team use the planning time?
- How were the plans made? Was your original plan successful?
- What changes did you make when you started to practice?
- Was your team successful in completing the challenge?
- Did you improve your time when the timed round was repeated?
- If you were to do this activity again, what would you change?

"So What" Questions
- What can we learn from this activity?
- What can this activity teach us about working together?
- If you become frustrated when working with a group, what can you do to lessen the frustration?
- Why isn't our first idea always the best way to solve a problem?
- What does the term "brainstorming" mean?
- How does brainstorming help us solve a problem?
- Did you look at other teams to get ideas? Would that be cheating?

- Where would you go to get help when trying to solve a problem?

"Now What" Questions
- How does working together help us solve problems?
- If you fail the first time you try something, what can you do to improve your chance of success?

TIME AND YOU

TOPIC AREA: Respect, Responsibility, School to Careers

CONCEPT: Time plays a number of important roles in today's fast moving society. One aspect of time is the act of being on time. We show respect for others when we respect their time. If we have agreed to meet someone at a certain time and do not show up at the appointed time, we are basically saying that what they have to do is not as important as what we are doing. It is our responsibility to be aware of our schedule and to keep an eye on the clock. At the workplace you are expected to arrive and be ready to go to work on time. Planning ahead and being on time goes a long way in convincing others that you are a responsible individual who respects others.

Being on time for an appointment or at the workplace is not the only area where time plays a factor. Meeting a deadline is also part of being responsible. When you miss a deadline it impacts others who are counting on you to complete your part of the job before they can finish what they have to do.

METHOD: Classroom activity

TIME ESTIMATE: 5 minutes plus discussion time

MATERIALS NEEDED:
• Watch with a second hand

ACTIVITY: Have everyone stand up and face you. Explain that they must raise their right hand and hold it as if they were being sworn in at a court of law. Next have them close their eyes. Their challenge is to see how close they can estimate when a certain amount of time has passed. For example, you tell the group that each of them are trying to estimate when twenty-five seconds has passed from the time you say begin. When they think the proper amount of time has passed, they are to open their eyes and clench their hand into a fist and immediately open it up again. This is the signal to the teacher that they believe the correct amount of time has passed. This is a motion that can easily be seen by the teacher. The movement is also subtle enough that it will not be detected by others, thereby alerting them to someone else's guess.

So they can tell how close they were to the correct time, you will count down from five seconds before the right time to five seconds after the right time. You cannot count out loud because this would give away the time to those who still have their eyes closed. To let them know, you will hold five fingers up and count down from five seconds before the correct time and then count back up to five seconds past the right time. When they open their eyes, they should look at you and see what the count is at that time. Once you have counted more than five seconds past the correct time, you can tell everyone to stop and open their eyes. Have them report out how well they did. You can do this by asking for a show of hands for those that were greater than five seconds before, within five seconds before, right on the mark, within five seconds after the correct time and more than five seconds beyond the right time. Repeat this same process again with a different time. Use times that are longer than twenty seconds and vary them for each round.

For round three and four have them repeat the same process except have them repeat words or phrases during the timing process. Any list of words or phrases will do, the purpose is simply to provide a distraction during the timing phase which interrupts their internal timing process. To accomplish this, you say a word or phrase and have them repeat it out loud. Continue giving them words and phrases to repeat throughout the timing period. Vary the speed at which you give out the words or phrases so they have more difficulty trying to keep track of the passage of time.

DISCUSSION IDEAS:

"What" Questions
* How did your guesses compare with the rest of the class?
* Were your guesses usually high or low?
* Was it harder to guess correctly when you had to repeat words?
* What method did you use to try and keep track of the time?
* Did you change your strategy as we went along?
* Did your new strategy work better for you?

"So What" Questions
* Why is being on time important?
* What problems can be caused when one person is late for an appointment?
* How does being late show a lack of respect?
* Whose responsibility is it for you to be on time?
* How does our being late impact others?

- Why is being on time to class important?
- How does our missing a deadline hurt others?
- If you have a job and arrive late, what could some of the consequences be?
- What could some of the consequences be for missing a deadline at school or work?
- How does being on time make others feel that you are a responsible person?

"Now What" Questions
- What strategies can you use to help you be on time?
- How can being on time help you gain the respect of others?
- How does being on time and meeting deadlines help you at school and in the work place?

TRADING

TOPIC AREA: **Conflict Resolution, Working Together**

CONCEPT: As we try to solve problems between people, we must realize that the best solution is one where everyone comes out a winner. Instead of thinking that there must be a winner and a loser when trying to solve a problem, we need to change their thinking to how can we both be winners and still reach our goal. When everyone wins, everyone is better off. Of course this type of thinking is difficult in a culture that believes strongly in competition and the philosophy that "winning is everything" and of "being number one". Solving a conflict is easier when we don't have to worry about winners and losers, but only in meeting everyone's needs.

METHOD: Classroom activity

TIME ESTIMATE: 15 minutes plus discussion time

MATERIALS NEEDED:
- Each person needs five pieces of paper about half the size of a playing card

ACTIVITY: Before the activity starts you will need to get a set of five pieces of paper for each participant. Each piece should be about half the size of a playing card. This can be accomplished by cutting a sheet of 8_ by 11 paper into eight equal pieces. Each set of five should be numbered on one side with the following numbers, 1, 2, 3, 4 and 5. Only one number goes on each piece of paper. Take all of the papers and shuffle them randomly into one pile.

Explain to the group that the goal is to collect five cards with the numbers one through five on them. You do this by trading with other players. A trade takes place in the following manner. A player approaches another player and says "I need a three." The other player must give them a card, but they get to decide which card from their hand they would like to trade. It doesn't have to be the number card that they requested. They may choose to help them reach their goal or they may choose to give them a card that doesn't help them. Then the roles reverse and the person who was originally approached asks for a certain numbered card and once again the decision must be made whether to help the player or not. Once the trade is completed, they break apart and move on to another person and repeat the process. The winners are the first five people to reach the goal of holding all five of the correct cards. Once you have the correct sequence of cards, you move to the front of the room and stop trading. Emphasize to them that only the first five people with the correct cards will be winners. Give them about three minutes or so to complete each round. The number of winners and the times for each round can be adjusted according to the size of your group.

When you pass out the five pieces of paper to each person, distribute them number side down and instruct the participants not to look at them until told to do so. When everyone has their cards, allow them to look at what they have and begin the trading. If anyone has been given cards that are already the correct sequence, take three of their cards and blindly exchange them with someone else.

Collect all of the cards and redistribute them for round two. In round two the goal of the activity changes. Now the desired outcome for entire group is trying to see how many people they can get to have the correct set of numbers in their hand before time has expired. You must emphasize that for the group to win they must have at least half of the people holding the correct cards. No one is a winner unless they reach that goal. Everyone still makes trades with only one partner at a time and all the other rules remain the same.

DISCUSSION IDEAS:

"What" Questions
- How successful were you in the first round?
- How many winners were there in the first round?
- Did you help those you traded with in the first round to get what they needed to win? Why or why not?
- How many winners were there in the second round?
- Did you help those you traded with in the second round to get what they needed to win? Why or why not?

"So What" Questions
- What approach to the game did you have in round one? In round two?
- Why did more people reach the goal of having all five cards in the second round?
- How did your attitude change when the goal for round two was announced?
- What type of atmosphere did having only a few winners in round one create?

- How did this atmosphere change when the group was trying to get as many winners as possible?
- How can having a win - win attitude help solve conflicts?
- What can this activity teach us about conflict resolution?

"Now What" Questions
- Why should we try to find win - win solutions to our conflicts?
- How does a "me first" attitude impact our ability to solve a conflict?

UNIQUELY ME

TOPIC AREA: Self-Esteem, Team Building

CONCEPT: Kids don't get many opportunities to talk about their own lives. That's too bad because many kids don't realize how unique they are until given a chance to share their lives with others. By providing a structured opportunity, you are giving them that chance. The statements they will write during the activity are affirmations that they do indeed have some unique or interesting aspects of their lives. Participants will also become aware of things about other people in the group that they were never aware of before. It will become apparent how many things we actually have in common.

METHOD: Classroom activity

TIME ESTIMATE: 15 minutes plus discussion time

MATERIALS NEEDED:
- 1 piece of paper for each person
- 1 pen or pencil for each person
- A watch with a second hand

ACTIVITY: Give everyone a piece of paper. Have them write down five statements about things they have done in their lives or abilities they have. They should try and choose things they think few other people have done. Each statement must start with the phrase "I have" or "I can." Examples would be "I have ridden an elephant", "I have gone to Disneyland", "I have broken my arm", "I have hit a home run", "I can juggle", "I can roller blade backwards", "I can stand on my head", etc. It would be best if you go over some examples aloud as a group before you have them start writing. This way they will better understand what you are looking for.

After they have finished writing, explain that they will now find a partner. Once they have chosen a partner, one person will read their first statement and the other person will declare if they have ever done what has just been read. If they have, then they receive ten points. If they haven't done what the person read, then the person reading their statement is the one that receives ten points. After the first person has read their first statement and their partner has answered, then the other person reads their first statement and the first person answers. The teacher will tell them when to find a new partner. Encourage them to talk about the statements until the teacher tells them that it is time to switch. Do not give them too much time. Watch the group and judge the time accordingly. About fifteen to twenty seconds seems to work for most groups. Each person now finds a new partner and they go on to statement number two and repeat the process. Continue this procedure until they have gone through all five statements. No one may partner up with the same person twice. Report out the scores for each person at the end of the activity.

DISCUSSION IDEAS:

"What" Questions
* How many points did you score?
* Which statement of your own do you think was the most interesting?

- Which statement of someone else's did you find interesting?
- Name something that you found out about someone else that you didn't know before.

"So What" Questions
- Is getting to know what someone else likes or dislikes important? Why or why not?
- Is sharing your own likes or dislikes with others important? Why or why not?
- What happens when others get to know more about you?
- What happens when you get to know more about others?
- How does sharing interesting parts of your life make you feel?
- Does everyone have unique things that they have done or can do?
- Is being unique a desired characteristic in our society? Why or why not?
- Do you want to always be unique? Why or why not?
- Is it good or bad to have the same abilities as someone else? Why?
- Why would you want to have some things in common with other people?

"Now What" Questions
- What are some good ways to get to know more about other people?
- What are the benefits of sharing who we are with others?

WE BOTH

TOPIC AREA: Diversity, Team Building

CONCEPT: People have a lot more in common than we generally think. Most people have a number of shared experiences, likes, dislikes and desires. Often we spend so much of our time arguing over our differences that we forget to recognize and celebrate our similarities. By focusing on the things that divide us, we set ourselves up for conflict and disagreement. If instead we were to focus on what binds us together, we could find common ground on which to enjoy and work with one another.

METHOD: Classroom activity

TIME ESTIMATE: 10 minutes plus discussion time

MATERIALS NEEDED:
- 1 pen or pencil per team of two
- 1 piece of paper per team of two
- A watch with a second hand

ACTIVITY: Have everyone get a partner. Give each team a piece of paper and a writing utensil. Explain that they will have two minutes to find things that they have in common. The items may not be physical characteristics such as we both have two eyes or are wearing shoes. Examples of the things they are looking for would be: "We both have flown in an airplane", "We both been to a summer camp", "We both like pepperoni pizza", "We both live in a two story house" and "We both have been outside of the United States". The object is to get the longest list of things they have in common within the time period allowed. They must write down at least one word on their paper that will represent each thing they have in common. When time has expired, have each team report out how many things they found that they have in common. Now have each group look at their list and report out the most unusual thing that they have in common.

For round two, have each team join with another team to make a foursome. Repeat the activity trying to find what the four people all have in common. Once again allow the groups two minutes to make their lists. They do not have to use only the commonalties they listed in the first round. They can explore new topics and areas. When time has expired have them report out how many items they found in common and the most unusual item.

For round three have two groups of four get together and repeat the activity again. Allow about two and a half minutes for this round. Once again have them report out how many items they found in common and the most unusual item.

DISCUSSION IDEAS:

"What" Questions
- How did you find out what you had in common?
- How did your group compare with the other groups in the number of common items in rounds one, two and three?
- Which of the unusual items did you find most interesting?

- If you had more time, would you have been able to find more things in common?

"So What" Questions
- What can this activity teach us about each other?
- How can knowing more about each other help us feel connected?
- How can knowing more about someone keep disagreements between us to a minimum?
- What happens when we concentrate on our differences instead of the things we have in common?
- Explain this statement: "Everyone is different but also the same."

"Now What" Questions
- What can we do when we meet someone who seems different than we are?
- How does having things in common help us work together?

WHERE'S MY GROUP?

TOPIC AREA: Cliques

CONCEPT: There are very few situations in a young person's life that are more traumatic than being left out of the "in group", however the "in group" is defined at the moment. This wanting to belong is so strong that we see kids getting mixed up with groups that they may not really want to be a part of - but they are desperate to be a part of something. This is where some of the interest in gangs has come from in recent years. Kids moving into a new school or city are especially vulnerable to any group that will reach out and make them feel wanted.

Cliques can be positive or negative, but the feeling of wanting to belong somewhere is so powerful that many times individuals don't consider the consequences of belonging to various groups. Being accepted is enough for them. If people can't get accepted into any group, sometimes they will form their own. This group may take on a form that is definitely outside of the mainstream school population. This occurrence can lead to other problems within a school.

METHOD: Classroom activity

TIME ESTIMATE: 5 minutes plus discussion time

MATERIALS NEEDED:
- 1 small piece of paper for each person

ACTIVITY: This activity needs at least ten people to really make it work. You will need one small piece of paper for each person involved in the activity. Before the activity begins, you will need to write on each piece of paper. You may write sayings on the papers such as "The moon is made of green cheese", "Humpty Dumpty had a great fall", "Ring around the rosies", "The Eagle has landed", etc. It really doesn't matter what the papers say. When you are filling out the pieces of paper, make sets of one, two, three and four. This simply means that you will write the same saying on one, two, three or four sheets of paper.

Pass the papers out face down to your students. When everyone has their paper, have them turn it over and silently read what it says. Tell them not to share what is on their paper with anyone until instructed to do so. Now tell them to get up and move around the room. Without talking, they are to show their paper to one person at a time. When they find someone who has the same saying on their paper as they do, then they work as a team to see if they can find anyone else who has the same saying. Give them enough time that everyone will have found their group. Announce to the class that time is up and that you want everyone who is in a group of two or more to go to the front of the room. Obviously there will be people without a group since you wrote some sayings on just one piece of paper. At the end, have the entire room clap for those people who found their groups.

If possible, you should set this activity up so that the people who will end up without groups have enough self-confidence that this will not be a threatening experience for them. One simple way is to make a small mark on the back of the "single saying" pieces of paper and as you pass them out, make sure that you choose these individuals with care.

DISCUSSION IDEAS:

"What" Questions
- How hard was it to find your group?
- How many were in your group?
- How did it feel when you found someone with the same saying?

"So What" Questions
- What can this activity teach us about cliques?
- How did it feel when we clapped and you were in a group?
- How did it feel when we clapped for those who were in a group and you weren't one of them?
- What is a clique?
- Are cliques good or bad? Explain.
- List the different groups that are found in your school.
- How do some people feel when they are not in a group?
- Does everyone want to be a part of a group? Explain.
- What are the advantages of being in a group?
- Are certain groups such as Cheerleaders, Jocks, Nerds, etc. stereotyped as to how they act?
- What are the stereotypes and are they true?

"Now What" Questions
- How can you help the clique problem?
- How can you help people who seem to have no where to belong?
- What should we do when a new person enrolls at our school?

TNT IDEA: Instead of using random or nonsensical saying when writing your phrases, use motivational quotes or facts from a unit that you are studying.

WHO TO BELIEVE?

TOPIC AREA: Decision Making, Media Influence, Peer Pressure

CONCEPT: We make decisions all of the time. But on what information do we base our decisions? Where do we get our information to make informed decisions? We must be sure that the people we listen to have credible information rather than incredible information. Do they have anything to gain by leading us astray? On what basis do we determine who to listen to and who to ignore? What role does trust play when accepting advice from others? Does the media always tell the whole truth?

METHOD: Classroom activity

TIME ESTIMATE: 10 minutes plus discussion time

MATERIALS NEEDED:
- 1 blindfold for every three people
- 5 small pieces of paper for every three people

ACTIVITY: Before you begin the activity, use one piece of paper per letter and spell out the word "right". Repeat this until you have enough spellings of the word "right" for each team of three. Now divide your group into teams of three. Give each team a blindfold and a set of papers that spell the word "right". Blindfold one team member and instruct them that their job is to spell out the word "right". Assign the roles of correctly helping the speller and incorrectly helping the speller to the other

two members of the team. These two helpers may verbally give advice and encouragement regarding the
placement of the letters. They may not touch the letters.

Do not let the blindfolded person know which helper
will be giving them the correct advice and which one will
give them incorrect advice. Allow approximately sixty
seconds for the blindfolded person to spell "right". After
time has expired, have the spelling checked. Repeat the
process for two more rounds so each person has experienced all three positions. Rotate the teams after each
round so the same people don't keep working together. If
the blindfolded person spells the word correctly, they
receive 100 points and the person who was helping them
spell it correctly gets 100 points. If the word is spelled
incorrectly, the person who was telling them wrong
receives 100 points.

DISCUSSION IDEAS:

"What" Questions
• How many points did you get during the three
  rounds?
• Which of the three positions did you enjoy the most?
  Why?
• Which of the three positions did you enjoy the least?
  Why?
• What strategies did you use to determine which
  helper to listen to?
• What strategies did you use to get the speller to
  believe you instead of the other helper?

"So What" Questions
• How can we compare this activity to making a decision?

- How do we determine which people to listen to when asking for advice?
- How much influence do our friends have on the decisions we make?
- How much influence do people we really don't know very well have on the decisions we make?
- What role does peer pressure play in making decisions?
- What are some decisions we make where we welcome input from others?
- What are some decisions we make where we don't want input from others?
- Is input from others always helpful? Explain.
- What role does trust play when getting input from others?
- Does the media always tell the whole truth?
- How do advertisers try to influence what you think?

"Now What" Questions

- What should you do before taking advice from someone?
- Why is input from others sometimes helpful when making a decision?
- How can we help prevent peer pressure from forcing us into a poor decision?
- How can we tell hype from fact when dealing with the media?

TNT IDEA: Blindfolds can cause problems. Just have the students close their eyes or cover their eyes with one arm.

YOUR HEALTH – YOUR CHOICE

TOPIC AREA: Alcohol and Drugs, Decision Making, Healthy Lifestyles, Tobacco

CONCEPT: We make choices about what goes into our body and how we treat our bodies. The kinds of things that we choose to ingest or inhale has an influence on our health. Not only do these things influence how healthy we are, but they can also influence how long we live. Decisions that we make can either shorten or increase the length and quality of our lives. There are many factors that play into a person's health. Some of these factors include age, body shape, heredity, genetics, etc. Therefore, not everyone reacts the same way to the same things. Everyone knows someone who is really old and yet has been smoking cigarettes for years. Even if the kids do not know the answers to the questions before you conduct the activity, it is a great awareness activity which lets them begin thinking about the fact that the decisions they make as a young person will help determine the health of their bodies as they grow older.

METHOD: Classroom activity

TIME ESTIMATE: 15 minutes plus discussion time

MATERIALS NEEDED:
- 1 pen or pencil per person
- 1 piece of paper per person
- Signs that say "A", "B" and "C"
- Masking tape

ACTIVITY: Give everyone a writing utensil and a piece of paper to keep their score on. Explain to the group that you are going to have them choose which items will have a greater negative or positive influence on their bodies. Each time you read them a question, you will give them three choices. Assign a place in the room for each choice. Hang signs to designate where they will stand for A, B and C. After you read each question, the students will go stand by the letter that reflects his or her choice. You will then read out the correct answer. The people who have chosen the correct answer will receive ten points. The numbers after each item listed is the number of calories, fats or calories burned. Do not read these numbers to the students until after they have made their choice.

- Round one: Which of the following foods has more calories in a serving? 2 Twinkies (300), 1 Powdered Donut (200) or 2 Ding Dongs (370)

- Round two: Which of the following substances harms the liver the most? Alcohol (correct), Tobacco, Marijuana

- Round three: Which of the following foods has more fat grams in a serving? Corn Dog on a Stick (10) Beef and Bean Burrito (13) 4 Chicken Nuggets (4)

- Round four: Which of the following exercises burns the most calories in an hour? Bowling (204) Jumping Rope (681) Roller Blading (477)

- Round five: Which of the following substances harms a person's short term memory the most? Tobacco, Methamphetamines, Marijuana (correct)

- Round six: Which of the following foods has more fat

grams in a one ounce serving? Doritoes (7), Pretzels (1) or Fritos (10)

- Round seven: Which of the following exercises burns the most calories in an hour? Bicycling (340) Jogging (477) Swimming (545)

- Round eight: Which breakfast item contains the most fat grams? Egg McMuffin (12) Sausage McMuffin (23) 3 Pancakes with syrup and 2 pats of butter (16)

- Round nine: Which of the following substances harms the lungs the most? Alcohol, Tobacco (correct), or Cocaine

- Round ten: Which of the following foods has the most calories? Banana (101) Apple (96) Orange (87)

- Round eleven: Which of the following foods has more fat grams in a serving? Arby's Regular Roast Beef Sandwich (19) McDonald's Big Mac (31) Burger King Whopper (40)

- Round twelve: Which of the following substances is responsible for the most deaths per year? Alcohol, Tobacco (correct), All illegal drugs combined

Have everyone report their scores to the group.

DISCUSSION IDEAS:

"What" Questions
- How did your score compare to the rest of the group?
- Were you mainly guessing or did you have a pretty good idea of why you made your choices?

- Did other people influence your choices?
- Which category did you have the most trouble with: calories, fat grams, exercises or harmful substances?

"So What" Questions
- Can you always tell how healthy a person is by just looking at them?
- Why do some people not show the effects of an unhealthy lifestyle?
- Do the effects of an unhealthy lifestyle always impact a person right away? Why or why not?
- How much influence does heredity play on how we look?
- How much influence does heredity play on how healthy we are?
- How do our daily choices affect the health of our bodies?
- How does the media influence the decisions we make about our bodies?
- Why do some people take chances with their health by using harmful substances?

"Now What" Questions
- Whose responsibility is it to keep our bodies healthy?
- What are some ways that we can keep our bodies healthy?
- How can we help others to keep their bodies healthy?

TOPICAL INDEX

Visit the
Active Learning Foundation's Web Site

www.activelearning.org

The Active Learning Foundation is a non-profit corporation that is dedicated to helping individuals, families, organizations and communities help themselves through education and skill building. Tom Jackson is the founder and director of the Foundation. Here is a brief summary of what you will find there.

Speaking Information: Check here if you are considering having Tom Jackson come to do a workshop for your group or present at a conference. You will find his vita, costs, travel needs and letters of recommendation along with descriptions of the various topics that he addresses.

Activity Books: Each of Tom's activity books are described along with pricing and ordering information. Also available are the covers of each book and some sample activities.

Teacher's Corner: Check out some activities and research that might be useful.

Parent's Corner: See what activities and research might be helpful for you to use within your own family or as part of a parent training program.

Funny One Liners: Nothing here but fun stuff.

Newsletter: Here you will find the latest research concerning how kids learn and active learning. You will also find information concerning workshops, new books and other resource information.

Real Life Stories: People who work with children and youth have shared their success stories regarding active learning.

Educators, Counselors, Youth Workers and Others: *Hear Tom Jackson Live!*

That's right! Wouldn't it be great to have Tom come to your school or conference and share with you his creative, yet practical hands-on activities? Tom's activities have been described by teachers and others who work with children and youth as "Simply the best life skill activities I have ever used! They teach life skills in such a way that kids not only learn, but love doing them." Or you can broaden the topic by having Tom talk about active learning as a teaching tool which can energize any classroom or program.

Reading about the activities is exciting, but there is no substitute for experiencing them. Tom uses his "learn by doing" approach to walk you through a number of activities from his books. Here is a chance to ask questions, get insider tips and learn first hand how to process and discuss the activities with your kids. Hundreds of teachers, counselors, youth workers and others have participated in Tom's workshops, and one of the most common remarks is, "I wish we had more time. This is the most useful workshop I have ever attended."

Tom is available for keynote presentations, conference breakouts, workshops, teacher in-services, peer helper trainings, youth leadership programs and conferences. Funding sources that have been used successfully by other organizations include staff development, Safe and Drug Free Schools, Title I, At-Risk and High Risk, as well as special grants and community resources. Join up with a neighboring school, school district or organization and save money by sharing travel costs when Tom stays more than one day in your part of the country. We will even try to book another workshop in your area to help you save money on travel if you will give us other likely people to contact!

Give Janet Jackson a call at (888) 588-7078 and ask for Tom's speaker packet. Or, just give Janet a call and suggest to her a person in your school district or organization who would be interested in hearing more about Tom and she'll contact them directly.

Parents, Parenting Instructors,
Parent/School Organizations and Others
Who Are Interested In Helping Families:
Invite Tom Jackson To Your Area

Help families help themselves! Invite Tom Jackson to make a presentation to the parents in your area. Tom doesn't conduct the usual parenting workshop where someone tells parents how they should parent. Instead, he gives parents easy to do, hands-on activities that can be done right in their own homes to open up the lines of communication and discuss important topics with their children in a non-threatening way. Tom also conducts workshops specifically for parenting instructors which focuses on how to facilitate parent trainings using Tom's activities.

Explore the values of caring, cooperation, honesty, perseverance, respect, responsibility, and service to others along with other topics. Rather than telling you what to believe, the activities provide a user-friendly vehicle to allow each parent the opportunity to share their own values with their children and have fun at the same time.

Reading about an activity is exciting, but there is no substitute for experiencing them. Tom uses his "learn by doing" approach to let you participate in a number of activities from his book *Activities That Teach Family Values*. Here is a chance to ask questions, get insider tips and learn first hand how to use the activities to discuss values with your kids.

Tom is available for keynote presentations, conference breakouts, workshops and evening presentations. These can be done for parents, trainers of parents or others who work with families. Another option is to conduct a workshop for parents and their children ages 7 to 15½. Have them actually experience the activities together and see how much fun they really are!

Give Janet Jackson a call at (888) 588-7078 and ask for Tom's speaker packet. Or, just give Janet a call and suggest to her a person in your school district or organization who would be interested in hearing more about Tom and she'll contact them directly.

Other Activity Books
By Tom Jackson

Don't miss out! Be sure that you have all of Tom's powerful, hands-on activities that you can use immediately to make a real difference in the lives of kids.

These activities will create excitement and increased learning anywhere there is a group of kids. Thousands of professionals have successfully used these activities with elementary and secondary groups and have found them effective with inner city, suburban, rural, high-risk and at-risk populations. These fun, hands-on activities have been tested in the real world of classrooms, after school programs, churches, prevention programs, treatment centers, juvenile detention centers, etc.

Students learn best by doing! All of Tom's books contain user-friendly activities that get kids involved in their own learning process and let them have fun at the same time. The books include opening chapters on how-to use activities and tips for leading effective discussions. Each activity is followed by a list of questions that can be used to help you transfer what you did during the activity to real life applications. These activities can be used in classrooms, counseling and support groups, youth programs, after school programs, churches or anywhere else you would find a group of kids. Great for all grade levels!

Activities That Teach

60 hands-on activities that address topics such as alcohol, tobacco and drug prevention, and which teach skills related to communication, values, working together, problem solving, stress management, goal setting, self-esteem, decision making and more. 234 pages. Retail price: $15.95 (Case discounts available)

More Activities That Teach

All different activities than Tom's first book. 82 additional hands-on activities that address topics such as alcohol, tobacco and drug prevention, and which teach skills related to anger management, resisting peer pressure, diversity, violence and gang prevention, communication, values, working together, problem solving, stress management, goal setting, self-esteem, decision making and more. 341 pages. Retail price: $18.95 (Case discounts available)

Activities That Teach Family Values

52 new activities that can be used by parents, character education programs, small group sessions, church groups or after-school programs to help adults stop preaching to kids and start sharing with them instead. Once again Tom's hands-on approach is used to address topics such as caring, cooperation, honesty, perseverance, respect, responsibility, service to others and much, much more. 217 pages. Retail price: $14.95 (Case discounts available)

Conducting Group Discussions With Kids

A leader's guide to making an activity meaningful and educational! Discover a simple, yet effective four step discussion outline that is effective and engaging. Additional strategies include getting kids to talk, questions to ask, discussion formats to use, room arrangement, teacher tips, student behaviors and much more. 120 pages. Retail price: $12.95 (Case discounts available)

For ordering information about any of Tom's books:

Call toll free (888) 588-7078
between the hours of 7:00 a.m. and 7:00 p.m. Mountain Time

▶

Write: Active Learning Center

3835 West 800 North, Cedar City UT 84720

FAX: 435-586-0185

web site: www.activelearning.org

e-mail: staff@activelearning.org

MasterCard, VISA, Checks, or Purchase Orders gladly accepted